Wedding Cakes Aren't
Just Desserts

by Sallia Bandy

authorHOUSE®

AuthorHouse™
1663 Liberty Drive
Bloomington, IN 47403
www.authorhouse.com
Phone: 1-800-839-8640

First published by AuthorHouse 07/01/2011

ISBN: 978-1-4567-3527-2 (sc)
ISBN: 978-1-4567-3528-9 (ebk)
ISBN: 978-1-4567-3529-6 (hc)

Library of Congress Control Number: 2011902703

Printed in the United States of America

Introduction

When I made my first wedding cake as a junior high student in 1969, there was no internet; only a few books, Mailbox News, and other cake decorators. There were no structured classes at the local craft store. My first class was taught by a lady at the local bicycle repair shop. Much of the knowledge in this book came the hard way and through studying and talking with others. Never underestimate the importance of networking with other cake decorators, either online at one of the multitude of cake decorators' social media web sites, at a day of sharing, during an ICES convention, or in a class. You can always pick up a tip. You might not know what to do with the tip at the time, but write it down and tuck it away, for you will find a way to apply it in the future.

This book takes the process of creating a wedding cake from the initial consultation with the bride through the delivery of the cake. It is designed for home bakers, culinary students, small business owners, and anyone who makes wedding cakes. As wedding cake artists, we are good at making tasty, beautiful cakes. But how we treat the customer throughout the process says a lot about us. We can be firm without being domineering, nice without being a pushover. Brides do have a choice of whom they want for a cake designer, and professionalism and great customer service tip the scales every time.

There are many fine books on the market with pictures of beautiful cakes to inspire us to reach the next level. Pour over those books for your design vision; then come back to this book to find out how to meet with a bride, present yourself, and where to find business cards.

Sallia Bandy
September 2010

Table of Contents

Consultation and Cake Tasting

First Impressions Count!

The consultation and cake tasting meeting is probably your first opportunity to meet the bride in person and make a good impression. It may also be your last chance. This is your time to set the tone of the consultation, so pay attention to these tips from sales professionals about making a good first impression:

- ✓ **Be ready to meet on time.** Make sure you are organized and can easily locate all of your support material - samples, brochures, pricing information, business cards, etc.

- ✓ Demonstrate **good listening skills.** Be interested in what the other person has to say; encourage them to talk and don't interrupt. Give positive verbal cues by asking questions that encourage conversation and put your bride at the center of attention. Control the conversation, but do not monopolize it. It's just as important to listen. Maintain eye contact and be friendly, yet professional. Don't offer solutions before making sure you understand your customer's needs. Ask questions before making recommendations.

  Three points of active listening are:
  - ✦ Keep an **open mind.** You won't like every design that you are contracted to create.
  - ✦ **Paraphrase** what you hear the customer saying. Don't parrot what she says, but rephrase in your own words to promote understanding.
  - ✦ **Take notes.** Don't rely on your memory.

- ✓ Present a **professional and polished appearance.** A neat, clean appearance will go a long way, so save the cutoffs and t-shirts for the beach. How you dress shows how important the customer is to you.

✓ Bring a **positive attitude** to the meeting. Smile and give your customer a solid handshake. (Don't overpower her.) Show your confidence by having good posture and an upbeat, friendly approach.

✓ **Speak well** and avoid words that you cannot handle. People judge us by the way we speak and present ourselves. Speak so that you can be heard – don't mumble, but enunciate clearly. Display animation in your voice and facial expressions to add interest to your words. Practice in front of a mirror or with someone you trust to build your speaking skills. Be careful not to use slang or words such as yeah, uh-huh, and okie-dokie. Never curse! Be professional. Practice with others or in front of a mirror.

✓ **Establish rapport.** Your bride has probably been given a lot of advice from friends and relatives about how she should plan her wedding, and not all of that advice may be accurate. Wait until you have conversed a bit and established rapport before challenging a statement she might make.

✓ Be careful with **humor.** Don't crack a joke or make a quip at someone's expense. You never know what might offend someone. 'Funny' comments could damage the trust you are building with your client.

✓ Use your **clients' names** frequently. This serves to help you remember their names, keep the conversation focused on the bride, and show that you paid attention when you first met.

A business relationship starts with the first meeting. Take time to **prepare**, be **professional**, establish **trust**, and your business relationship will be fruitful for everyone: you gain a client while your bride gains confidence in your abilities.

While I mention the bride in consultations and designing, the groom often plays a larger role in the wedding cake today. Very often, it's the groom who has the design ideas and thoughts as to how the cake(s) should look. The groom is no longer relegated to just showing up at the wedding!

Closing the Sale

Your bride is meeting with you to buy a service. You can make the event a pleasant and even memorable time, but your goal is to close the sale. Here are a few closing tips to help you during the consultation:

- Expect to get the sale. Have a positive attitude.
- Avoid rushing the closing process. Listen!
- Remember to directly ask the customer for his or her business.
- Be as specific as possible when outlining closing actions or steps. Do you have a contract to sign? What deposit do you require? What methods of payment do you take?
- Avoid talking too much during the closing. Listen!
- Do not keep selling after the sale has been made. Finish paperwork, get the client something to drink, thank her for her business.
- Avoid closing gimmicks. Follow-through and deliver what you promise. This will be the best advertising.
- Ask for agreement from the customer. Make sure that you have heard what she needs.
- Communicate confidence through your voice when closing.

A Picture is Still Worth a Thousand Words

Your portfolio is your story. It represents your creative works of art captured via camera, and then quickly eaten (very willingly by the wedding guests)! A portfolio can be anything from a collection of pages in a binder with pictures of your cakes to an elaborate scrapbook or, perhaps, a digital display.

Photographing Cakes

The first rule is: take pictures of each one of your cakes. You can't get them back after they're eaten without recreating them, which means hours of work. The digital camera has made the task of capturing your work a dream, because you can take many pictures from all angles, save the ones you want, and delete the ones you don't like. You also have the gratification of seeing how your pictures will turn out immediately, without having to wait for film to be developed. Before digital cameras, I used a 35mm camera, developed my film, and sometimes discovered that none of the pictures were very good. By then, it was too late – the cake was long gone. When I bought my first digital camera, I was thrilled that I could take thirty pictures and know that at least a few would come out perfectly.

Here are a few tips for taking pictures of wedding cakes:

+ **Lighting** plays an important role in your photo. Use lighting and shadow to make the cake look three dimensional and give it texture and life. Look at the cake from different angles and turn lights on and off to determine your best shot. Since your flash can wash out the cake's design, stand further away, zoom in, and try to shoot with light coming from the side. This will give your cake depth and the flash will be far enough away to not wash out your subject.

+ **Compose** the photo. Remove distracting background objects and arrange the cake in the most photogenic way possible—perhaps even moving the table nearer to a useful source of light. Light

5

candles on the table for a nice effect. Arrange the toasting glasses near the cake and take the picture from different heights.

+ Use a **tripod** if your hands are shaky or when taking long-range shots. When using the zoom on your camera, your body movements are exaggerated, which can cause blurry shots. One way to prevent blurry pictures is to buy a camera with built-in image stabilization and make sure it's turned on for your shots.

+ **Partner** with the photographer hired for the wedding. Ask the bride during the consultation who the photographer is and contact them. Offer to give them credit for the photograph that you use in your portfolio and they may give you the photo for free. Be sure to include their name on the photo and refer them to brides who are looking for a photographer.

Create a Scrapbook

You are creative and spend many hours on a wedding cake. Why shouldn't you display the cake in the most creative way? There are many resources to help you get started in scrapbooking, from supplies at your local craft store to instruction in the form of books, classes, and the internet. You can find scrapbook pages in all colors and patterns, as well as die cuts, buttons, stickers, ribbon, lettering, and many more embellishments. Use scissors with patterned blades to display your photo uniquely and punches to create easy decorations. Keep in mind that the picture of the wedding cake is the point of the page, so keep your scrapbook professional, not overdone. Also, digital scrapbooks are becoming more and more popular, so don't limit your creativity to only the print medium.

Digital Portfolios

There are many ways to create a digital portfolio. You can insert all of your photos into a Microsoft PowerPoint™ presentation and run a slide show to present your work. A slide show can be controlled by the viewer or configured to run automatically. The latter is good to set up in your showroom by using a flat panel monitor and desktop PC or laptop. It provides art for your space, while serving a business purpose of advertising your cakes.

You can use Windows Media Center to create slideshows of your photos as well.

There are many FREE internet photo sharing sites that you can use to display your cake photos. Some photo sharing sites are Atpic, BlueMelon, Flickr, Fotki, Imageshack, Imgur, Interartcenter, ipernity, Jalbum, Kodak Gallery, Mobile Me, Panoramio, Photobucket, Phanfare, Picasa, Piczo. com, SmugMug, Snapfish, Shutterfly, Webshots, Wikimedia Commons, Woophy, and Zooomr.

See the Resources section of this book for links and other suggestions.

Digital Picture Frame

You can use a digital picture frame to display a slideshow of your cake photos in your showroom, at cake shows, and at bridal shows. It's easy to change the photos and add more. Most frames allow you to connect a USB drive to hold even more photos. Visit www.cnet.com or www.zdnet.com and check reviews and prices of popular digital frames.

Simple Binder

Insert your photos in page protectors and arrange them in a binder for an easy, low cost, effective portfolio. As your bride browses through the book, encourage her to remove pages of the cakes that attract her attention. This is especially helpful if the bride doesn't have any idea of what she wants. As the pictures grow on the table, you will see common threads – stacked cakes, monochromatic themes, simple, frilly, etc. This will help you design a cake that is uniquely her.

Photo Album

Buy a nice photo album and arrange your pictures to tell your story. Photo albums have non-acidic paper and plastic protective sleeves or page coverings to keep your portfolio clean and undamaged.

Photo Books

Photo books are easy to create and a great professional alternative to photo albums. The books are bound collections of your best photos, ready for browsing and presentation. You can have them created anywhere photos are developed – drugstores, supercenters, and online. Photo books come in hardcover, paperback, leather, linen, and many other styles. Because the photos are reproduced from digital images by high-end equipment, your cake photos come out beautifully. Very often, you can find photo books at the same websites that will allow you to upload photos for display. Check out the Resources section for contact information.

Getting Started

If you haven't done many wedding cakes and don't have a large portfolio, use pictures from the internet, books, or magazines. *Make sure that you can actually make the cake pictured.* If you have never used rolled fondant, don't offer it on a cake until you have completed several rolled fondant cakes. (Practice on your family, neighbors, and coworkers.) Once you master a cake, replace the magazine photo in your portfolio with your own cake photo. You will find that soon all the pictures will be your own works of art.

Tasting the Cake

This is the bride's favorite part of planning the wedding – tasting lots and lots of cake, icing, and fillings. While this can be overwhelming, a good cake designer can guide the bride to make the right choice. There are two reasons for a bride to taste the wares of a cake designer: to ensure that the cakes, icings, and fillings are of high quality; and to narrow down flavor(s) of cake for her wedding. When serving cake to taste, make sure it is the same as you would bake for an actual wedding cake. The same goes for the icing and fillings. If you use seedless raspberry filling at the tasting, use the same filling in the wedding cake.

There are several ways to present cake to the bride for sampling, so pick the one that works best for you. If you have a shop with assistants, you might hold group tastings on a regular schedule. However, if you are the only one creating the cakes, a group tasting might not be practical.

Group Tasting 'Party'

Many cake designers schedule open cake tastings in their showroom so that brides can sample cakes without a formal consultation. These events are usually free and include coffee and tea to complement the cakes. If you hold them as an open house, no one may show up, so have the brides make reservations. If they don't show up, you still have contact information for advertising to them. Pick a slow business day for these tasting parties so that you can be available for questions. You can conduct the tasting and explain your business, or let the brides choose what they want to sample. Set out samples of cake (sheet cakes cut into 1" x 2" pieces work well), icing, and filling and let the brides mix and match to create their own flavors. Cupcakes can be used, but are more informal. Provide forms for them to make notes on what they have tasted, including your contact information, hours, prices, or any other advertising you would like the bride to remember.

You can create sample cakes, including filling and icing with your most popular flavors or whatever you have on hand from your baking. As you bake the necessary layers for your wedding orders, make extra 6" round cakes for tastings. Torte, fill, and ice a single layer; then complete it with simple decorations. Precut the cakes into 1" wedges and let the brides serve themselves. When cut into 1" wedges, a 6" cake will yield 18 servings.

The bride can make a reservation for a private consultation at another time, or if you have ample staff to cover the group tasting, hold the consultation during the party. Make sure you have a separate room for privacy.

Private Tasting and Consultation

Private tasting and consultation should be scheduled by appointment. Most cake designers set aside thirty to sixty minutes for each appointment, with a break in between, so that brides' appointments don't overlap. Some designers charge for the tasting and apply the fee paid for the tasting to the order if the wedding cake is booked. If you find that prospective clients are booking appointments and not showing up or cancelling at the last minute, you might want to collect a tasting fee up front to discourage this behavior. Another good rule of thumb is limiting the number of people who can accompany the bride to the tasting. More than two or three additional people tend to confuse things more than help, so be clear in your advertising, and when setting up the appointment, about how many people can attend the tasting.

There are several ways to conduct the cake tasting. When the bride calls for an appointment, ask her which two to four flavors of cake and fillings she would like to taste from your menu or offer her flavors that you are baking that week. Depending on your business volume, you may or may not have a number of cake flavors on hand. Offer your most popular flavors and don't spend hours baking tasting cakes that may sit in the freezer too long and be wasted.

Your business and customer service skills will come out during a cake tasting, so keep everything professional. You may serve your award-winning cake and the bride may make a face after tasting it. Don't comment. Not everyone will like your favorite cake and others may rave about one of your cakes that you don't particularly care for. Your goal is to serve the best possible cake you can make, and figure

> Be professional. Listen and clarify to understand. Your **reputation** is your greatest asset.

out what the bride wants. I once served a white cake with strawberry filling (pretty plain in current wedding circles) and the bride made a comment about it tasting like a "peanut butter and jelly sandwich." I remember thinking that there was not the slightest hint of peanut butter anywhere near the cake, but made a note of it anyway. When she tasted the mousse and Bavarian cream fillings, she loved them. What I learned from that experience was that this bride loved creamy filling and not fruity ones, but couldn't express that until she had tasted the cakes.

I learned a simple trick from my friend, Jennifer Bartos, about creating clever tasting cakes. Make extra 6" x2" round cakes when you do your normal baking. Cut the layers into halves, thirds, or fourths, depending on how many flavors you have. If you have four 6" cakes of four different flavors, cut each cake into fourths. This work is more easily done if the cake is frozen. Then torte each cake quarter and arrange four quarters on a cake board with a doily. (You can also cover the board with foil or use a greaseproof cake circle.) Pipe a narrow dam of icing around the perimeter of the round cake and over the cut edges. Fill with one or more fillings to compliment the cake flavors. Label the cake board to indicate the cake flavor and filling for the bride's reference (and yours!) Top with the matching four cake sections, ice, and add a simple decoration. I keep extra royal icing flowers, chocolate decorations, or sugar pieces on hand to top off the cake. This gives the bride her very own cake to taste and take home for other members of her family. It also gives you three additional unique tasting cakes for your future wedding tastings. Be sure to wrap the cakes well or put each in a zipper freezer bag for storage and they will keep, un-iced, for about 6 weeks (Duncan Hines) .

Other options for serving cake for tasting are:

+ Serve small circles or squares of cake along with dishes of fillings and icings. Let your bride and groom make their own flavor combinations to see what they like. See Figure 1 for an example. The wedding party will have fun mixing and matching flavors and will remember you when it comes time to make a decision as to who will win their business. You can send leftovers home with the bride for others to taste.

+ Serve your most popular cake, filling, and icing combinations cut from a tasting cake. You can freeze most iced and filled cakes to keep on hand.

+ Serve cupcakes or mini cupcakes. You can fill them by inserting a plain or star tip into the cupcake and squeezing a small amount of filling into the center. Top them with your popular icings.

Figure 1 - Let the bridal party create their own cake, filling, and icing combinations by offering help-yourself servings.

The Consultation – Ask the Right Questions

You've met the bride and made a good first impression. Now it's time to get down to business and find out what she wants. Ask questions to determine the bride's plans, style, and how grand of a reception she is planning. The following table lists some common questions to ask and why.

Table 1 - General Consultation Questions

Question	Reasoning
Name of bride and groom	Get both names to fully identify the wedding party. Other vendors may have the wedding recorded as the Smith/Jones party.
Mailing and email addresses of both bride and groom	To send invoices, reminders, and information.
Phone numbers	Get numbers from both parties (ex., home, work, cell). Get at least two numbers.
Wedding date and time	If the wedding is held at the same place as the reception, you'll want to deliver the wedding cake before the wedding, not the reception.
Reception date, time, and day of the week	The reception may be at a different location than the wedding and may be a party that occurs weeks or months after a destination wedding.
Delivery time	This can be determined closer to the wedding by the wedding coordinator or reception venue manager.

Question	Reasoning
Reception location and directions	Very important to have.
Reception contact and contact information	You'll need to coordinate delivery time. Be sure to get a cell phone, as main numbers may not be answered on weekends or nights.
Will the cake be located inside or outside?	Consider the time of year. Many icings will not hold up to hot summer temperatures.
How many guests are expected to attend?	Used to size the cake.
What food will be served? A full dinner? Buffet? Hors d'œuvres? Only cake and punch? BBQ? Will dessert be included or is the cake serving as dessert?	The more food, the less cake you may need. Ask probing questions about the amount of food being served. People will tend to eat more wedding cake if only cake and punch are served, as opposed to a large BBQ with cobbler.
What drinks will be served?	If this is a big beer-drinking crowd, you'll need less cake, as the two don't mix very well.
Will there be a groom's cake?	A groom's cake can be the same size as the wedding cake or as little as half the size. It depends on the bride's wishes.
Do you have any pictures of cakes that you like?	Sometimes, brides will see pictures on the internet, in books, or in magazines. It doesn't hurt to have this information when designing a cake.

You may want to know other details of the wedding including, but not limited to, the photographer, the florist, and the person responsible for returning deposit items, and/or the person responsible for payment.

Taking the Order

Use an order form to work through questions asked of the bride, so that you don't leave out any critical details. See Appendix K for an example of an order form. Also have pens, pencils with erasers, graph paper (Appendix J), the Cake Sizing Charts (Appendices A, B, and C), and a calculator handy.

Ask the bride if she has any pictures or ideas for her cake. She may have brought a swatch of fabric, a bit of lace, paint chips, or even a picture of the details on her shoes she wants copied or reproduced. If the bride has an idea about the cake, you can start with that. Ask her if she is partial to a certain shape; such as round, square, hexagonal, or other. Coupled with the number of servings, you can begin determining the basic shape and size of the cake.

Sometimes the bride has purchased a cake topper or is using one handed down in the family. Ask her to bring the topper to the consultation as it may give you ideas about the direction of the design.

If the bride doesn't know what she wants, have her flip through your portfolio while you are beginning the order and looking at possible cake sizes. (See Appendix A – Bride's Cake Serving Chart and Appendix B – Groom's Cake Serving Chart.) I have the bride pull pages that she likes out of the binder so that we can look at them to determine common factors. Some brides pull out three pages and some pull out twenty. Even with that number, you can find similarities and narrow down her likes and dislikes. I ask the bride, at this point, what she likes or dislikes about each picture and make notes.

After you have determined the size, shape, and general structure of the cake, use the graph paper to begin a sketch. Draw the cake proportionally, using the graph paper as a guide. This will show you whether your cake configuration will work.

Estimate the cost before you go any further. (See the chapter *Running a Cake Business* for more details on determining costs and pricing.) The bride will have a figure in mind for a cake, so ask if the cost is in her budget. Being up front in this budget discussion will avoid problems later. If the estimated cost is not in the bride's budget, several things can be done to reduce the cost of the cake.

Table 2 - Reducing Cake Costs

Adds Cost	Lowers Cost
Rolled fondant	Basic icing
Gumpaste flowers	Icing, real, or silk flowers

Adds Cost	Lowers Cost
Large wedding cake	Smaller wedding cake with sheet cakes
Complex decorations – lots of piping and hand work	Simple design
Elaborate cake stands, fountains	Stacked cake
Individual cakes	One cake

At this point, you can work on the design. Since this is such a big topic, I devote an entire chapter to it later. For now, let's say you have worked with the bride through all the requirements and come up with a design she absolutely loves.

Finish the order as to the number of servings; number, shape, and size of each tier; as well as icing type and color, cake flavor, filling, type of flowers, fountain, fountain cascade, water color, ornament or cake topper, and deposits and rental fees.

Deposits and Rentals Fees

There are several deposits that you will want to charge on the wedding cake order:

Table 3 - Types of Deposits

Item	Charge	Refundable/ Nonrefundable	Reasoning
Book the date	Most shops charge $25 to 50% of the cake price	Nonrefundable	Depending on how many wedding cakes you do in a day, you are turning away business when someone books a date. If they cancel the wedding cake, you should be compensated for the loss of business.

Item	Charge	Refundable/ Nonrefundable	Reasoning
Cake stand or plateau	Charge at least replacement cost for expensive cake stands and plateaus.	Refundable upon return of items in good condition	If you don't charge a deposit, the customer has no incentive to return your items.
Fountain	Charge replacement value.	Refundable upon return of items in good condition	If you don't charge a deposit, the customer has no incentive to return your items.
Plates, pillars, bridges, stairways, etc.	Charge replacement value or build the cost into the cake price so that the bride doesn't need to return the items.	Refundable upon return of items in good condition	If you don't charge a deposit, the customer has no incentive to return your items.

Take pictures of items you want returned and leave a printed version when you deliver the cake. This will help ensure that you get back what you are expecting. You'll probably get back everything that comes out of the cake, including dowels, cake circles, and flower picks, as brides want their deposit back!

Rentals fees can be charged for fountains, cake stands, cake plateaus, and any other items that will be used. A fair rental price as of this writing is one-fourth to one-half the cost of the item. A $100 silver cake plateau might command a $25-$50 rental fee.

Contract

It is important to put everything down in writing for your protection as well as the bride's. Sample contracts can be purchased from legal forms web sites, but it's best to have your lawyer review it to ensure that it is valid in the area in which you live. By signing the contract, the bride agrees to the design and details of the cake and such details as payment arrangements and cancellation dates. The cake designer's signature gives the bride confidence that there will be a wedding cake at her wedding and it will look like the one that was designed at the consultation for her.

A contract may include the following items, but the list is by no means exhaustive for everyone's situation. Contact your lawyer if you have questions about what to include in a contract.

See Appendix K for an example of a simple contract.

1. General description of the 'project' – the service(s) being contracted
2. Description of the design and details
   a. Comprehensive list of details of cake
      i. Cake flavor, fillings, and icing
      ii. Number of tiers and shape
      iii. Number of servings
      iv. Decorations, such as flowers and cake topper
3. Completion timeframe or due date – term of the contract
4. Contact information and notices
   b. Vendor contact information (florist, venue, caterer, photographer)
      i. Name of business, address, phone number
      ii. Emergency contact number for day of wedding
   c. Client information
      i. Bride's and groom's full names, addresses, phone numbers
      ii. Alternate contact
      iii. Wedding date and time
      iv. Location for delivery
5. Any general legal provisions
6. Who will provide what equipment and decorations
7. Payment amounts, arrangements, and refund policies
   d. Total price
   e. Due date of balance
   f. Deposit for rental items and cost if not returned in specified condition
   g. Delivery and set-up fees
   h. Cancellation date – last date to make changes
   i. Penalties if client cancels and last date to cancel without forfeiting entire cost
   j. Policy if cake designer cancels

  k. Gratuities

  l. Deposits

  m. What is refundable or not

  n. Type of payments accepted – cash, check, credit card

  o. Returned check policy

  p. Reimbursable expenses

8. Rental item and items to be returned information

9. Date and signature of bride and/or groom

10. Date and signature of cake designer

Cake Design

A wedding cake is an architectural work of art, personalized to the tastes of the bride and taking into account the logistical details of number of servings and construction. You must design and build a beautiful cake like an exquisite building – wonderful to look at and sturdily built. Unlike a building, however, the cake must taste wonderful. Wedding cakes can be simple or extravagant. One of Queen Victoria's cakes in 1840 is said to have measured three yards in circumference and weighed over 300 lbs. (Royal Collection Department of the Royal Household, 2007).

There are many things to consider when designing a cake. You need to think ahead to delivery, how to execute that special design the bride wants, how to avoid construction problems, and many more. Here are a few things to think about before you sign that contract...

- ❖ Will the design work? Is it top-heavy? Does it require sculpting or undercutting that will make it unstable? Will you need to use Styrofoam pieces in the construction?
- ❖ How will you transport it? Does it have a large base? Can you get it out the door? Have you checked the reception site to ensure you can carry it in their door? Does it have a center column? Pillars? How will you move it safely?
- ❖ If there are fresh flowers, how will you construct the cake so that the flowers don't stick directly in the cake or touch it?
- ❖ What will the weather be like? Are you using a nice Swiss meringue buttercream in 98°F heat?
- ❖ If you are using a fountain, is the cake big enough to look proportionally correct?
- ❖ Will you make your own gumpaste pieces or purchase them?
- ❖ Have you accomplished this design before or will it be new to you? Will you need to allow extra time to practice the techniques?

Basic Cake Designs

The following pictures represent basic cake styles. These can be adapted to any shape of cake (round, heart, square, etc.) and can be built on a centerline or offset.

Figure 2 - Stacked Cake

Stacked

The stacked design has remained very popular throughout wedding cake history and was probably the first design that evolved from early wedding celebrations – a stack of cakes.

The supports for this style are hidden inside each tier.

Separated

Separating the tiers of a cake gives it height and makes it seem larger.

You can use the space between the tiers in your design to add flowers, a cherished ornament, initials, or other design element.

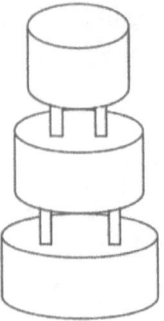

Figure 3 - Separated cake

Combination

Stacked and tiered cakes are combined to achieve this look. The top tier is easily removed for saving.

This design will also add height to the cake and allow for design elements between the tiers.

The supports for the middle tier are hidden in the bottom tier.

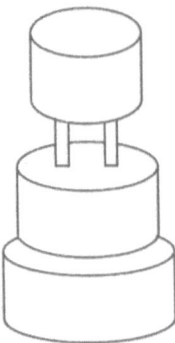

Figure 4 - Combination stacked and separated cake

Satellite

Using satellite cakes with the main cake increases the numbers of servings, allows for different flavors in each cake, looks large on the table even if the cakes themselves are not big, and each cake is easy to serve.

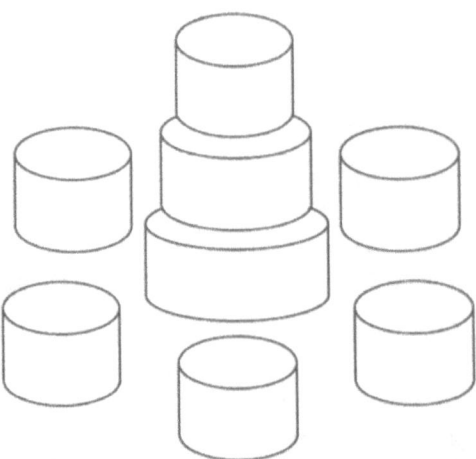

Figure 5 - Stacked cake with satellite cakes

Cake Styles

Traditional

What is traditional? If you married in England, your idea of traditional may be fruitcake with marzipan and royal icing. In America during the 1950's, traditional was a monochromatic, stacked cake with icing roses and sugar bells. Before you assume a cake picture in your head when the bride says she wants a traditional cake, ask her to describe what she has in mind. White cake is an American tradition, because the pound cake lost its British fruit due to scarcity of ingredients in the new colonies. Recipes were commonly called "White Cake," providing a sharp contrast with the so-called "Black Cake" [fruitcake] (Charsley, 1992).

Classic

A classic cake style is monochromatic in white or ivory, three stacked tiers, and in a round shape. The cake flavor is usually white, with white buttercream icing. If color is used, it is kept to a minimum and usually in pastel tones. The borders and side decorations are piped, usually delicate vines, swags, string work, and shell borders. The cake topper is either the traditional bride and groom or a more updated grouping of flowers.

Figure 6 - Traditional white cake with sugar bells

Figure 7 - 2-tier traditional cake in light ivory

Contemporary

Contemporary cakes are designed for the wishes of the bride and are creative works of art. They may be multicolor or monochromatic, covered with rolled fondant or buttercream icing, and contain any flavor cake and filling. They could have multiple flavors of cake with decorations of dots and/or dragees. They may even be monogrammed and decorated with drapes and bows. Fruit is often used to decorate the cakes, especially sugared fruit. The possibilities seem limitless.

Cake flavors can be whatever the bride desires: from white cake and buttercream, to spice cake and cream cheese icing. Some of today's luscious cake flavors include Italian cream, dark chocolate, carrot, and strawberry sponge. Pair these cake flavors with any of these tasty fillings – white chocolate mousse, Bavarian cream with fresh strawberries, Grand Marnier, or tiramisu cream.

Figure 8 - Monochromatic fondant cake with fondant embellishments

Figure 9 - Monochromatic buttercream cake with flower embellishment

Whimsical or Thematic

These cakes use color and may incorporate lace designs on the bride's cake, resemble a stack of gift packages, or even luggage. Whimsical cakes are topsy-turvy colorful stacked cakes that look as if they defy gravity. As with contemporary wedding cakes, flavors can be simple or exotic, such as coconut key lime cake and mango mousse filling, or dark chocolate truffle cake and Kahlua mousse filling.

Figure 10 - Whimsical cake

Non-cake Ideas

Believe it or not, not everyone likes cake. Popular trends have introduced cupcake towers, cookies, brownies, cheesecake, candy, individual cakes, table cakes, croquembouche, dessert bars, etc.

Cupcakes

Cupcake towers and displays have become popular for several reasons. Each guest can help themselves to their own, personally decorated cupcake, so there's no need for someone to cut and serve cake. Some brides have opted for a traditional wedding cake and then serve decorated cupcakes to the guests. Add a menu to the display as shown in Figure 11 and guests can choose from different flavors of cupcakes. Cupcakes are less formal than traditional wedding cakes, but work very well in an outdoor garden setting. Imagine a tower of 200 cupcakes covered with different colored flowers to top off a spring garden wedding.

Figure 11 - Cupcake tower with flavor menu

Cookies

Cookies make great favors to give to wedding guests. Individually-packaged, decorated cookies can be made to match bridal colors, laces, monograms, and/or themes. Cookie cutters come in many wedding shapes: bell, bow, bride, groom, wedding cake, heart, cross, wedding dress, wedding ring, cupid, champagne glass, and many more.

Brownies

Brownies and bar cookies are popular alternatives to wedding cakes and cupcakes. You can decorate each one with a flower or monogram and use a cake stand to display them.

Figure 12 – 2-tiered cake surrounded in cookies and topped with gold-wrapped candy

Cheesecakes

Cheesecakes are popular as wedding cakes for the bride who doesn't like cake. You can ice and stack them to look like a traditional cake, pile on chocolate-covered strawberries on separated tiers, or cover with fondant as a gift package.

Candy Decorations

Candy can be used to decorate a cake to give color, whimsy, and an additional treat for the guests. Surround a simply-iced cake with peppermint sticks and tie it up with a pink or red ribbon and bow for a dramatic look. Candy can also be custom-made for favors and table decorations. Wedding lollipops are popular and candy molds can be found in many shapes and sizes.

Individual Cakes

Individual cakes are a very personal way to share wedding cake with guests. Because of the time that you spend on each individual cake, your price will go up proportionately. It will take as much time to make and decorate individual cakes as it will for several large wedding cakes. Figure this time into your prices. An individual cake can run anywhere from $15 to $50 depending on your location within the country (ex., cakes cost more in Boston, MA, than in Bozeman, MT) and the complexity of the cake. The cakes can be made in several different ways: tiers cut from sheet cakes like petit fours, then stacked and iced; small multi-tiered cake molds where you bake all the tiers at once; cookies stacked together with icing; and one-tier single serving cakes.

You can decorate the individual cakes just like their full-sized cousins, only using smaller tips and flowers. Make the flowers ahead of time from fondant, gumpaste, or royal icing, so that you can decorate the cakes in an assembly-line fashion. Cover the baked cakes in poured fondant, pourable chocolate, rolled fondant, buttercream, or any favorite icing. The easiest way to ice the tiny cakes is with a cake icer tip (#789) fitted onto a 16" or 18" pastry bag. Simply put the cake on a turntable, hold the tip next to the cake, then squeeze, spinning the cake table slowly. You can have a textured effect with the ridged side held toward you and a smooth effect with the ridged side held against the cake. This method is quicker than icing with a spatula and you avoid the frustration of trying to ice such a small cake.

Table Cakes

Table cakes can be used with or without a main wedding cake. Each table is decorated with a centerpiece featuring an 8" or 9" cake that serves the number of people at the table. The pricing is somewhere between a large wedding cake per slice and individual cakes. One benefit of the table cake is that the bride has a ready-made centerpiece and can combine the cake budget with the centerpiece budget. Add some gumpaste or real flowers and she has saved on her centerpiece flower budget as well.

At one wedding, I created fourteen 8" table cakes to serve ten guests per table. Since there was to be no main wedding cake or groom's cake, the bride decided to make one layer white and one layer dark chocolate with a raspberry filling. The decorations were simple – a few flowers with stand-up chocolate piped initials. To make the cutting easier, I used ten rosettes as the top border. The bride and groom came to each table and cut the first piece of cake and greeted their guests personally. The guests enjoyed the surprise and there wasn't a long line for wedding cake. The bride and groom had their own 9" heart-shaped cake to cut in the traditional way.

Pastry

If individual cakes, brownies, or cheesecakes don't work for the bride-to-be, there are several other options for her. Croquembouche is popular worldwide and is a tower of bite-size profiteroles (choux pastry puffs filled with vanilla pastry cream) which are coated in a thin crust of crispy caramel. The "glue" which holds the puffs together in their stunning pyramid shape is caramel, melted toffee, or chocolate ganache. You can decorate them with gumpaste flowers, a delicate cake topper, or spun sugar surrounding the tower like a cloud. Instead of cutting the croquembouche as a traditional wedding cake, you strike the top with a hammer to break it up. One tradition was to have the bridesmaids catch the falling cream puffs in a tablecloth. There is a recipe for croquembouche in <u>A Sweet Quartet: Sugar, Almonds, Eggs, and Butter: A Baker's Tour, Including 33 Recipes</u> by Fran Gage (North Point Press, 2003).

Desserts Bars

Dessert bars or wedding dessert buffets are becoming popular with brides looking for variety and cost savings. You can have a smaller traditional wedding cake plus a tableful of sweets, ranging from cakes, pies, bars, candy, flans, soufflés, trifle, bite-sized desserts, cookies, petit fours, and/or fresh fruit. A chocolate fountain rounds out the setting and provides an elegant, but fun atmosphere.

The dessert table encourages guests to mingle, rather than stay seated at tables. If the bridal couple has favorite ethnic desserts, they can customize the table to include them as a personal touch. One small town near my home has a charming tradition where everyone in town comes to the wedding and the ladies of the town create a dessert table full of homemade goodies that rival any gourmet wedding cake. This community tradition celebrates the gift of sharing in honor of the bride and groom.

Totally Different Ideas

Finally, there are ideas that are so inventive, they deserve a separate paragraph! Imagine a cake made from stacks of donuts. Who wouldn't love that? How about a cake stand filled with Twinkies, HoHos, Snowballs, Ding Dongs, and fried pies? A junk food lover's dream!

A make-it-yourself ice cream sundae bar would go far at a hot summer garden wedding to cool off the guests. Don't leave out the children. Create a cookie decorating station where they can make the art and eat it too. Chocolate fountains are all the rage these days. Surround the fountain with pound cake, fruit, marshmallows, pretzels, potato chips, and more and let the guests serve themselves.

Design Inspiration

If a bride brings you a picture of a cake and asks you to copy it, that's easy (assuming you can execute the details). Coming up with a design that is personal to the bride is fun and sometimes challenging. You are the cake designer, so you need to guide the conversation to figure out what will work best. Without ideas from the bride, where do you get inspiration for a design? There isn't a wedding cake muse, so you're on your own for this.

Start with other people's cakes on the internet, in books, and in magazines. There are many pictures of wonderful cakes in these resources that can help you. You can adapt a design as it is, or you can apply designs to different tiers. Use polka dots from one cake and cornelli lace from another on two different tiers. It's OK to wear stripes and dots these days, so it's OK for the wedding cake too.

Ask the bride for a picture of her wedding dress. Use the dress designs and embroidery patterns to create one-of-a-kind piping on the cake. One bride brought me a photocopy she had taken of her dress with little beaded snowflakes and I copied the design on the cake in piping and dragees.

China patterns often inspire cake designs. There have been numerous publications and even a cake show that tied china patterns to wedding cake designs. The delicate trim of a china plate can easily transfer into piping on a cake.

The wedding flowers often give inspiration to wedding cake design. A cascade of gumpaste or real calla lilies down the side of a cake complete the picture when calla lilies are the main theme in a wedding bouquet.

Wedding gift wrap, wall paper, and the wedding invitation itself have lent scrolls, vines, hearts, and other delicate themes to the cake design.

Wedding locations can also serve as inspiration, e.g. seashells on a beach wedding cake, horseshoes and piped rope on a western cake, lots of flowers for a garden wedding, antique quilt designs for a wedding in the country, a castle for a Disney wedding, or bright colors for a fiesta-themed wedding in Cancun.

Topping the Cake

Traditionally, a tiny bride and groom stood watch over top of the wedding cake. Today, you can still have that bride and groom in many different versions – ethnic, military, comical, themed, or in animal form. Besides a standard purchased or handmade wedding cake ornament, flowers, bows, and initials are very popular. Flowers carry the theme of the whole wedding. Initials can be made of fondant, candy, pulled sugar, gumpaste, metal, or plastic and can be ornate or simple. Initials are readily available through vendors on the internet or at your local craft store in the wedding section. Remember the adage of "something borrowed"? You could use an ornament that has been handed down through the family. One couple's son made figures of the entire family out of clay (including the dog, the cat, and the hamster!) I used the figures in-between the bottom two tiers of their wedding cake, placing them on a mirror on the bottom tier.

Groom's Cakes

Background and Tradition

When wedding cake traditions came to America from Britain, the traditional wedding cake was a fruitcake. This translated into a white pound cake in America. White was often associated with the bride, so this cake became the Bride's cake and due to the pound cake's thinner layers, was stacked higher than its British fruitcake counterpart.

In the 1890's, a choice of cakes was common in America – a bride's or white cake and a groom's cake, which was usually a fruitcake. In *The British Baker* in 1897, the 'Plain Bridegroom Cake' was a white cake. It was cut by the bridegroom and served with a glass of wine to the bridesmaids before going to church (Charsley, 1992).

The groom's cake was a non-white cake (usually spice, carrot, chocolate, or other) that was stacked above the white bottom tier. The white tier was served at the wedding and the groom's tier was saved for the wedding couple. Eventually, the groom's cake was removed altogether and kept as a separate cake in several areas of the country. Supposedly, if an unmarried woman slept with a piece of the groom's cake beneath her pillow, she would dream of her future husband.

Groom's Cakes Today

There are numerous ideas about where the groom's cake originated and what purpose it serves. Today, in fact, the groom's cake can be a popular addition to customize the wedding. It usually represents interests or hobbies of the groom, including cars, motorcycles, sports teams, college themes, animals, military, music, or any other idea the groom may have.

Figure 13 - Groom's guitar cake

One of my favorite cakes was a picture of the groom's guitar that the bride sent me. I turned it into an edible image and designed the cake around it. The groom came into the reception as I was setting it up and did a double-take. He said it looked just like his guitar. When I said it was his guitar, he was thrilled. This was a memorable cake, not for its complexity (it was simple), but for what it meant the bride and groom.

Sizing the Cake

Serving Size

Most wedding cakes are priced by the slice or serving. This method gives the bride a basis for comparison when shopping for a cake designer. A serving of wedding cake is about half the size (or less) of a serving that you would serve at a birthday party or for dessert. If only cake and punch will be served at the reception, you might want to suggest bigger servings.

Figure 14 - Serving example

Keep a piece of Styrofoam handy to show the bride when you discuss servings with her, as it's difficult to imagine a serving size. The size of the Styrofoam example should be 1" wide by 2" long by 4" tall. This would show the average size of a two-layer cake comprised of 2" layers. If your cakes are a different height, or you would like to offer bigger servings, cut your Styrofoam example to match what you would like to use. If you make four layers instead of two (see Figure 14), designate them by coloring in the 'filling' area.

How Many Servings?

There are several factors which determine how much cake you'll need at a wedding.

- How many people does the bride expect to attend? Average attendance is between 50 to 75 percent of invited guests, so a good estimate is to size a cake for two-thirds the number of servings as there are invited guests (assuming that most invitations account for two people).

- How much food is being served? If it's a full dinner complete with dessert, you won't need as much cake. If dinner is a buffet and the wedding cake is serving as dessert, then plan on a piece of cake for everyone.

- What is being served to drink? Is the reception a BBQ with kegs of beer? You won't need as much cake, as beer and cake don't work well together.

- Will there be a dessert or candy table? If so, you will not need as many servings.

- If the wedding party discovers that not as many people showed up as expected, either cut the cake servings larger or send cake home with guests. As a cake designer, it helps to include some extra boxes in case there is cake to send home with guests. The caterer or hotel should have extra boxes as well for leftovers.

- You may need more cake if each tier is a different flavor. When guests realize that there is lemon cake with raspberry filling, they will go back for seconds. In cases like this, it's best to cut the cake up and make labels for the cake slices on the table so that guests can choose what flavor they want.

Big Cake, Small Wedding

Sometimes a bride will have her heart set on a cake design from the internet or a magazine, but she doesn't need very many servings. The room where the reception will be held should be taken into consideration as well. A large room with high ceilings will dwarf a small cake. Consider how the cake will look in the reception area. If the cake design will not scale down to a smaller size, you can boost the size of the cake in several ways:

+ Use a dummy cake as one or more tiers. Be sure to charge for the fake tier as you'll be putting almost as much work into it as the real cake tier. Ice and decorate the dummy tiers as you would the rest of the cake. If using fondant, apply icing, water, or piping gel to the dummy, so that the fondant will stick to it.

+ Use pillars to make the cake look larger. A stacked cake can look squat, so give it some height with pillars.

+ Raise the cake on a table by putting something sturdy (cinder block, glass rack, large Styrofoam dummy) on the table and scrunching fabric or another tablecloth over it.

+ Use glass bricks or blocks to raise the cake. This technique looks especially nice with white Christmas twinkle lights between the blocks.

+ Use a cake stand for ease of setup and to make the cake look taller.

+ Put two separator plates and pillars under the bottom tier to raise it off the table. You can use a fountain or flower arrangement within the pillars and plates to add a nice touch.

+ Instead of assembling the tiers one upon another, spread them out on the table, making use of different heights of glass racks or bricks as supports. Cover the supports with a cloth or tablecloth scrunched up to look elegant. Decorate the table with rose petals, ivy, wedding confetti, chocolate kisses, or any other décor that fits the wedding theme.

Big Wedding, Small Budget

Here are some ways to stretch the bride's budget. Working with the bride to accommodate her budget may win you the business over another cake designer who won't budge.

+ Make a smaller wedding cake with one or more sheet cakes to be served in addition to the cake on display. Divide the sheet cake into 2" x 2" squares and put a small flower onto each square serving. This makes the cake easy to cut with each flower decoration designating a serving.

+ Keep the decoration to a minimum. Choose a simple design which requires less work. Less work equals less cost. Many brides are opting for simpler designs today.

+ If you charge rental for stands and fountains, avoid them as they will add to the overall cost of the cake.

+ Serve the wedding cake as dessert after the meal instead of an additional dessert.

+ Fresh flowers can sometimes be a false cost-cutting measure as some flowers can be expensive at various times of the year. Talk with the bride about options: artificial flowers, and some types of sugar flowers, can be relatively inexpensive to make and use.

+ See *Table 2 - Reducing Cake Costs -* for more cost reduction ideas.

Stretching the Number of Servings

+ Increase the size of each tier. A 6-10-14 round cake serves about 95 where an 8-12-16 serves 135. You keep the basic shape of the cake, but increase the servings.

+ Use satellite cakes. A satellite cake is one that stands on its own around the main cake. This method:
  o stretches the number of servings,
  o is easy to serve,

o   lets you keep the design as planned on the main cake, and
o   makes a cake look large on the table.
Make sure you request a large table for this technique.

+   As well as stretching the budget, one or more sheet cakes can be added to serve in addition to the cake on display. Divide the sheet cake into 2" x 2" squares and put a small flower onto each square serving. This makes the cake easy to cut with each flower decoration designating a serving.

Sketching the Cake

During the consultation it helps to draw or sketch a picture of the cake so that both you and the bride have the same visual in mind when discussing the cake. The bride may be thinking lace like her dress, and you may be thinking cornelli lace, possibly two very different designs. The main reason you are meeting with the bride is to design a cake that meets her requirements. If you can't sketch her cake on paper, the bride will have little faith that you can replicate it in sugar. You could write a detailed description of the cake for the order, but the finished cake will be a visual art, so the best way to represent it now is as a picture.

You don't have to be an artist to sketch a cake for a bride. We often are hesitant to draw the cake because we think the picture needs to be a work of art itself. You don't have a lot of time in a consultation, but you can produce an accurate representation of the cake. Later you can fill in details and colors and meet again with the bride or email your sketch to her for final approval.

I use graph paper as it allows me to show the cake to scale, so I know whether or not the proportions of the tiers will work together (see Figure 15). This sketch will serve as your guide to building and finishing the wedding cake, so add descriptions of designs, ornaments, colors, borders, piping, fondant pieces, bows, etc. For a better representation, color your drawing with colored pencils or markers.

There is graph paper included in Appendix J for your use.

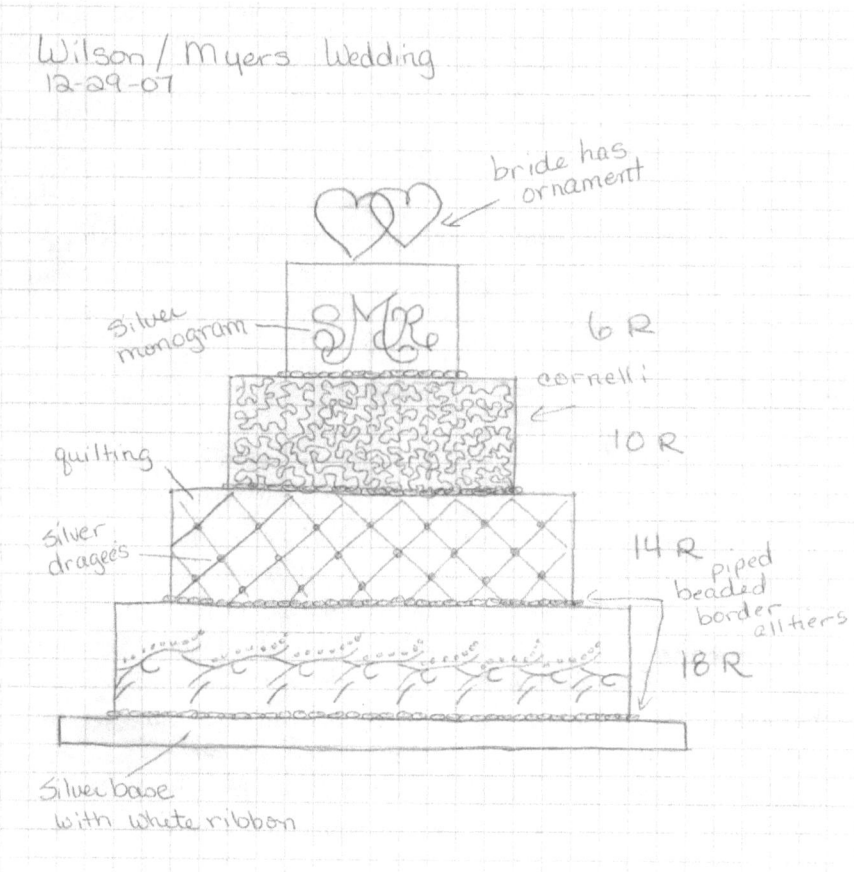

Wilson / Myers Wedding
12-29-07

bride has ornament

silver monogram

6 R

cornelli

10 R

quilting

silver dragees

14 R

piped beaded border all tiers

18 R

silver base with white ribbon

Figure 15 - Sketch of cake on graph paper

Here are a few things to remember about your sketch:

+ Use pencil! You can erase and change the design many times during the discussion.

+ Start with a center point and mark it on the paper. This way all of your tiers will be aligned if you are making a cake with a center alignment.

+ Fill in as many details as you need to finish the cake. Remember that you may have the consultation and draw the sketch six months or even a year before you create the cake, so the more details, the better.

- Use this drawing to make a shopping and to do list for the wedding cake. Include separators, pillars, support dowels, dragees, fondant pearls, etc.

- If using push in pillars, be sure to account for the part of the pillar that is hidden in the cake. If you have a 4" tall tier and 9" pillars, you'll only draw 5" above the cake, as 4" of the pillar will be hidden in the cake.

Construction Methods

Cake Stand

This is the easiest construction method as it requires no structure pieces inside the cake. Each cake tier sits on its own plate on the cake stand making it easy to disassemble and cut the cake, as well as transport to the reception site. I used this method on a boat prone to rocking in the wind and had no issues with stability.

Many cake stands come with plates that fit securely in the stand, so you run less risk of the cake toppling if the table is bumped. Stand manufactures recommend that you use a cake two inches smaller in diameter than the cake plate for ease of handling and stability.

The most creative ways to display a cake don't involve purchased cake stands. Bricks, telephone books, upside-down cake pans, Styrofoam cake dummies, sturdy dishwasher glass racks can be used under a draped table cloth or nice fabric to create a unique cake stand on the table. You can arrange the cakes in multiple levels to present a smaller cake and make it look larger. You can add confetti, rose petals, flowers, or mementos in the draping to personalize the wedding cake display.

> To keep cakes from sliding, put a piece of rubberized shelf liner, cut to fit, between the cake board and the cake stand plate.

Use a family heirloom to display the wedding cake. This could be a cherished silver tray or cake plate, or sturdy vase, on which the cake is placed. Sometimes the bride will bring a cake stand and ask you to design a cake around it.

Other creative ideas for cake stands are glass blocks with small white string lights, a themed stand (such as one contrived to look like a dock at a nautical wedding), or a custom-made stand. Visit Earlene Moore's website to view her fabric cake stand creations. The instructions can be purchased at her website for a nominal fee (Moore, 2007).

How to Use Cake Stands

1. Fill and ice your tier on the same-size cake board.
2. Use icing, double-sided tape, or rubberized shelf liner, attach the cake to the plastic cake plate.
3. Decorate the cake tier.
4. Transport the cake tiers and stand to the reception.
5. Place the cake in the stand so that the pegs on the bottom of the plastic cake plate fit securely inside the bars of the cake stand.

Figure 16 - A cake stand is easy to use and gives the cake a clean line

Cake stands can be decorated with ribbon, silk or real ivy, flowers, grapes, or just about anything you can think of. This incorporates items into your design that won't come in contact with the cake, but give the appearance of being part of the whole look.

Stacked

Cake tiers stacked one upon another can be simple in design or elaborate, tall or short, buttercream or rolled fondant. This traditional style is timeless and always in demand. You can make tiers of any shape and size – round, square, hexagonal, paisley, or mix- and-match shapes. Cake tiers can be thick or thin. You can trim the tiers so that they appear to sit on a slant or keep them level. There are so many options. This said, the support for a stacked cake is usually internal and that theory stays constant no matter the cake shape, size, or angle.

A tier on a stacked caked is not supported by the tier below it, even though it appears to be. Some form of dowel must be used to support the tiers and is imbedded in the lower cake tier. The dowels can be plastic, metal, wood, or other sturdy material. If you have a multi-tiered cake, remember that your lowest tiers must support the combined weights of the higher tiers. For example, if you are designing a four-tiered cake, the bottom tier must support the weight of the top three tiers.

What should you use for dowel supports in each tier? There are numerous types of supports made for internal use in the cake. Wilton makes a plastic dowel that is easy to cut yet very sturdy. A great product is the Stress Free Support System by Cakes, Inc. from South Dakota. This system is easy to use and very sturdy. There's no cutting required as the supports are adjustable making them work for any

> ◈ Do not use drinking straws for supports. You may end up with a one-tiered cake.

size of cake. From their website: "The Stress Free Cake Supports are a set of stainless steel discs with threaded bolts welded on the disc. Delrin legs are threaded onto the bolts forming a solid support to use to support your wedding cake design" (Stress Free Cake Supports, 2007).

All in One Bake Shop (see the Resources section) carries a dowel the diameter of a drinking straw but much stronger. You can cut it with scissors or a knife, and it takes up very little room in the cake.

How to Build a Stacked Cake

1. Ice cakes on the same-size cake circle.

   Note: Cover the cake circle in white or clear plastic contact paper to prevent moisture from soaking through and weakening the cardboard.

2. Put dowels in all tiers except for the top tier.

Measure the height of the tier with a skewer (Figure 17), then cut all of the dowels to that measurement. This will ensure that the next higher tier is level. Be sure to measure each tier as each, probably, will be slightly different.

Mark the tier with a cardboard circle the same size as the next higher tier. This will give you a 'target' when you place the next tier as well as a guide for placing the dowels.

3. Pick up the tier and place it on top of the prepared tier.

    You can put coconut, royal icing, or powdered sugar between the tiers to help the icing not stick when the tiers are separated.

4. Once all of the tiers are in place, and to stabilize the cake for transport, push a sharpened ¼" dowel rod down through the tiers. Sharpen the dowel rod with a pencil sharpener.

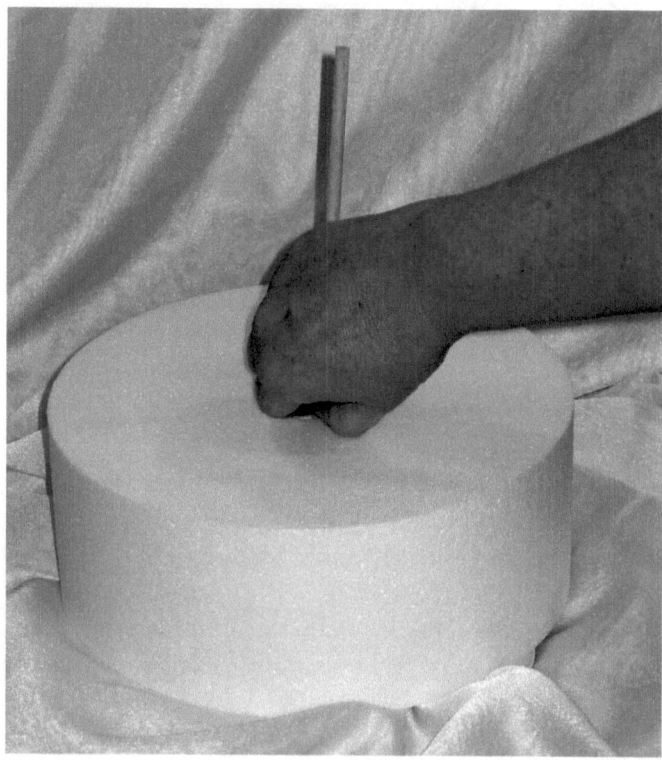

Figure 17 – Measure the height of the cake

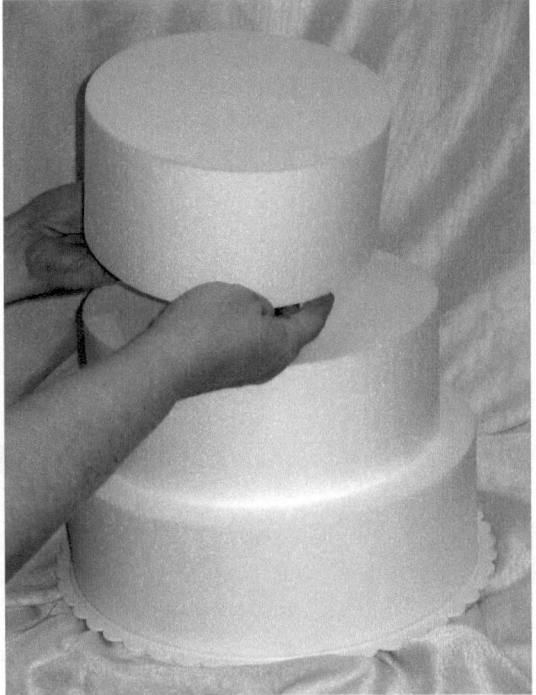

Figure 18 – Carefully set the tier in place

Push-in Pillar

This method uses one plate and four pillars. The cakes should be enough different in size that there is at least 1½" between the pillar and the edge of the cake. The cake must support the pillars; any less might cause the pillar to pull through the cake if jostled.

1. Ice cakes on the same-size cake circle.

   Note: Cover the cake circle in white or clear plastic contact paper to prevent moisture from soaking through and weakening the cardboard.

2. Mark the tier for pillar placement. Use the separator plate from the next tier above and gently press it onto the tier, feet down, making sure it is centered. When you lift the plate away, the feet will leave marks on the icing to mark the position of pillars. Repeat this procedure for each tier, except the top tier.

3. Place each tier on its separator plate, securing with icing, double-sided foam tape, or non-skid shelf liner.

4. Push the pillars straight down into the cake, using the marks as a guide, until pillars touch the cake board.

Figure 19 – Push the pillars straight in the cake

5. Start with the tier above the base tier and place the feet of the separator plate on the pillars.

6. Continue adding tiers in the same way until the cake is completely assembled.

    Transport each tier separately and reassemble the cake at the reception site. Leave the pillars in place for transport.

Two Plates and Four Pillars

Uses two separator plates and four pillars. The advantage of this method is that you can place flowers or other decoration on the plate between the tiers without them touching the cake.

Note: The connected separator plates need to be the same size.

1. Ice cakes on the same-size cake circle.

Note: Cover the cake circle in white or clear plastic contact paper to prevent moisture from soaking through and weakening the cardboard.

2. Set tiers on separator plates. The plates can be larger than the cake or the same size.

3. Mark tier for plate placement. Use the separator plate for the next tier above, gently pressing it onto the tier, feet up, making sure it is centered. Lift plate away. The plate will leave marks on the icing to guide the position of plate when you assemble the tier. Repeat this process for each tier, working from largest to smallest tier. Leave the top tier unmarked.

4. Insert dowel rods into cakes (see Stacked Cake instructions) and position separator plates with the feet facing up. Putting powdered sugar, coconut, or royal icing under the plate will help it pull off easier when serving. Otherwise, when you pull off the plate, you'll pull off all the icing too.

5. Position pillars on the separator plate feet.

Figure 20 – Position the pillars on the plate

6. Set cake plate on pillars. You can continue to add tiers this way. Check the proportions of the cakes and pillars. You might want

to use taller pillars on the bottom cakes and shorter pillars as you increase in height. It depends on the look you are trying to achieve.

Transport the cakes separately. Be sure to remember to take the pillars with you. I always add them to my checklist!

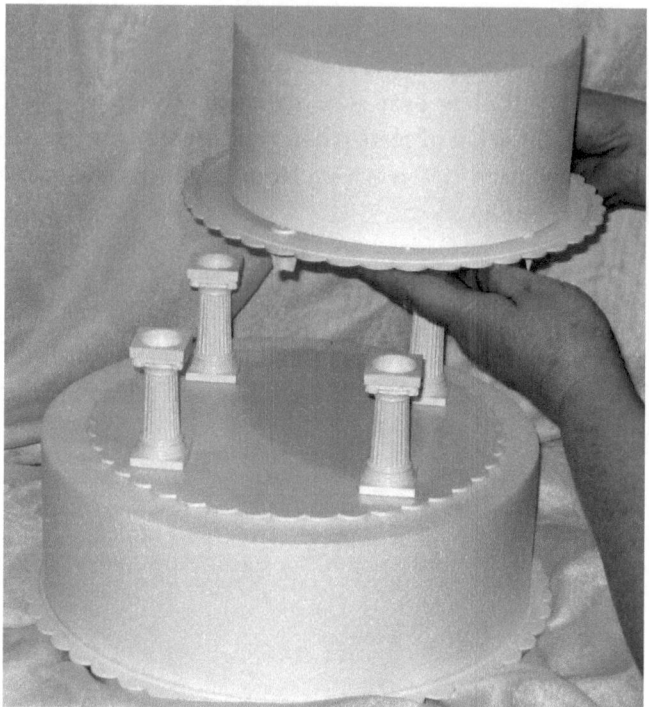

Figure 21 – Position the tier

Center Column Construction

This is another very easy way to construct a tier cake and there are numerous styles of center column stands available. The center construction cake configuration is great for tucking in flowers between the layers to hide the center support.

In the following directions, I'll describe the Wilton Basic Tall Tier Cake Stand which allows you to build a multi-tier cake. You can use all five plates, or fewer, depending on the size of your cake.

1. Cut cardboards to fit each of the tiers, if necessary.

a.   Make a pattern out of wax or parchment paper for each tier except the top tier.
b.   Fold the paper pattern in quarters.
c.   Snip the point to make a hole. Unfold and the hole will be in the center.
d.   Test the hole for size by slipping it over a column, making it larger if necessary.
e.   Trace the hole pattern on the cardboard and cut it out.
f.   Cut a hole in the top tier board to allow for the column cap nut.
g.   Save the patterns for marking the cake tops later.

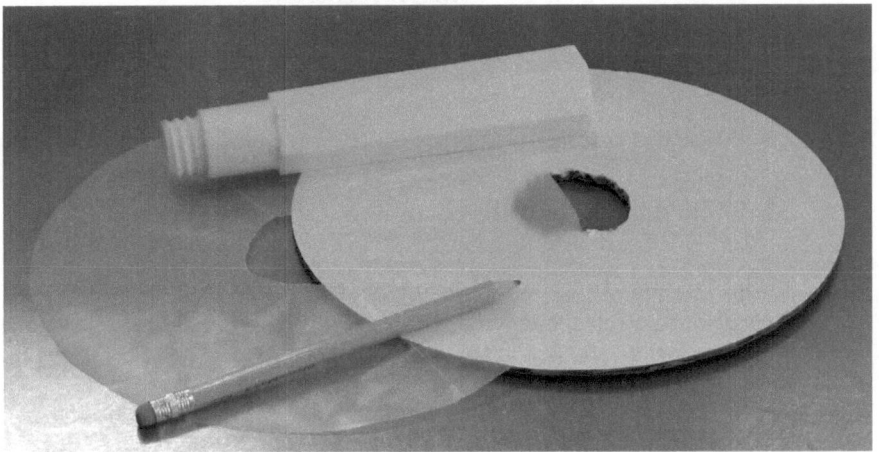

Figure 22 – Cutting the template

2.   Determine which plate will support your bottom tier and glue on the plate feet if necessary. Use strong glue designed for plastic.

3.   Ice cakes on the prepared cardboards (with the hole).

4.   Make the center holes in all cakes except the top tier.

h.   Mark the top of the cakes with the paper pattern. Use the pattern that corresponds to the cake size.
i.   Cut the hole by pushing the cake corer through the tier down to the bottom.
j.   Remove the cake corer from the cake. Plunge the upper part down to eject the cake from the cake corer.

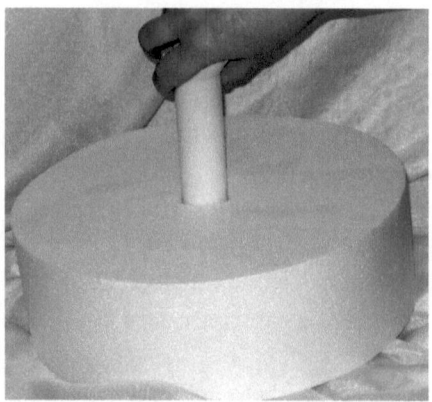

Figure 23 – Cutting the center core

5. Build the cake.

   k. Screw a column into place on the base plate (the one with the feet).
   l. Slip the cake over the column to rest on the plate.

   Tip: Because the plates dip in the center, you might want to add cardboard circles, cut with the center hole, but 1"-2" smaller than the cake to bring the cake up to the level of the outer edge of the plate. Otherwise, your cake may dip and settle in the center to conform to the dip in the plate.

   m. Set the next smaller plate in place on the column.

Figure 24 – Set the next smaller plate in place

n. Screw a column into place on the plate (no feet).

o. Continue to build until you get to the top tier.

6. When you get to the smallest plate that you want to use, add the plate and secure with the top column nut. Place the top tier on the plate. Make a mark (decoration or dot of icing) along the back so that you can align the tiers at the reception.

Transport each cake separately, and don't forget to take the columns with you. To transport easily, place non-skid shelf liner in a cake pan so that it hangs over the edge. Place the cake, still on the plastic plate, in the cake pan so that it rests on the shelf liner. For example, use an 8" round cake pan for a 10" plate and so on. You can also take the cakes off the plastic plates and transport all separately.

Figure 25 – Center column final

Fountains

Gently falling water turns a wedding cake into a spectacular display. Most fountains on the market also light up, so the look is stunning. Assemble all fountains following their package directions.

Very important! It is a good idea to test the fountain **BEFORE** the reception to be certain the water is flowing properly and the light works.

Be sure the display planned for the fountain will accommodate the height and width of the fountain. Measuring and assembling plates and pillars with the fountain ahead of time will prevent any unpleasant surprises at the reception if the fountain does not fit.

Because the fountain requires larger plates and pillars, a large cake looks best. If you have a small cake, consider using a Styrofoam dummy as the base tier.

You can also use the fountain on the table with the cake as a nice decoration.

1. You can buy a flower ring to go with most fountains. The ring holds flower arrangements in place and hides the mechanics at the base of the fountain. If using a flower ring, position the ring and fountain on the plate.

2. Assemble the pillars and second or top base plate.

3. Note: You must use 14" or larger plates and 13" or taller pillars for the tallest fountain cascade. Measure the height of the fountain you are going to use before you buy the pillars so that you will know what size to buy.

4. Assemble cakes as normal, setting the largest cake on the plate just above the fountain.

Stairways and Bridges

Stairways Without Bridge

Stairways make cakes look large and connect satellite cakes to the main cake. You can put flowers and bridal party figures on the stairs. Sometimes the little plastic people do not want to stand up, but a little double stick tape will make them comply.

Cakes with stairways are very popular for Quinceanera celebrations.

It helps to have at least two people to arrange the cakes with stairways.

1. Arrange main cake and any satellite cakes in position.

a. Hold the stairway above cake and adjust cakes if necessary. The points sticking out of the stairway insert into the main cake.
b. Insert points sticking out of the stairway into the side of main cake until the stairway is flush with side of the cake.
c. Rest the bottom of the stairway on the top of satellite cake.

2. Add more stairways, based on your design.

3. Add figurines or flowers.

If the figures or flowers are the least bit heavy, support the stairway in the satellite cake with dowels so that the stairway won't sink into the cake (or worse, tear the cake).

Stairways With Bridge (Use 2 to 4 Stairways, I Bridge)

It helps to have at least two people to arrange the cakes with stairways and bridges.

1. Arrange main cake and any satellite cakes in position.

a. Hold the stairway above cake and adjust cakes if necessary. The points sticking out of the stairway insert into the bridge.

2. Add more stairways, based on your design.

3. Add figurines or flowers.

If the figures or flowers are the least bit heavy and will rest on a cake, support the stairway in the satellite cake with dowels so that the stairway won't sink into the cake (or worse, tear the cake).

Baking the Cake

Beautiful AND Tasty

Wedding cakes can be beautiful and taste good! It's true! Don't let anyone tell you the opposite. You should take care in your baking, using the best ingredients to produce a delicious cake. If you want to make a new recipe, experiment weeks or months in advance. Don't wait until you are baking the actual wedding cake to find out that the recipe doesn't work or you can't execute it. Plan to do one or more trial runs if you have not made many wedding cakes. If you are using a new recipe, try it out on your family, friends, and neighbors first. They will be happy to help you test. Carry the dry run through to the completion and assembly of the wedding cake if possible. This will uncover any problems and give you a better idea of how much time to plan.

If you are using a mix, either retail or commercial, you can add ingredients to it to make it tastier, firmer, or tinted. Look on the inside of the cake mix box or on the manufacturer's website to see if there is a version of the mix that works best as a wedding cake. Usually, these recipes are firmer than a regular box mix. Some suggested add-ins for a mix are:

+ 1 tablespoon grated lemon or orange peel
+ 2 or 3 teaspoons vanilla, almond, orange, lemon, or other extract
+ Substitute coffee or orange juice for water
+ Substitute ¼ cup liqueur for the equal amount of water
+ Stir in grated chocolate, finely chopped nuts, coconut, poppy seeds, or well-drained fruit after the batter is prepared

Are you baking a large wedding cake? Pans greater than 14" to 16" may not fit in a home oven. Be sure to check your oven size with your pans **BEFORE** buying the pan, mixing the cake, and preheating the oven. You may need to bake the cake in half-rounds that will fit into the oven, and then stack them.

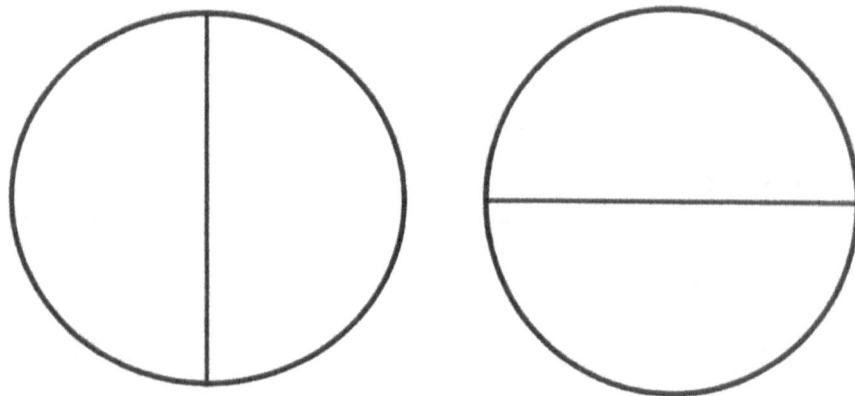

Figure 26 - Stack your half round alternately for better stability

For easier cake assembly, bake cakes several days in advance and store, well wrapped, in the freezer. (See Appendix H for a suggested timetable.) You can ice the cake frozen or thawed, but cold. If you are torting the layers, cut them before freezing and put a piece of plastic wrap or parchment paper between the layers, otherwise you will need to thaw the cake before cutting it.

Always start with perfectly level cakes. If your cake baked with a dome, cut it off with a serrated knife. You don't want your cake to resemble a basketball on the plate and it will not sit level with the hump. (In classes I'm constantly amazed how many people skip this step.) Cut the hump off while the cake is in the pan, using the pan as a guide, and you will have a nice, even cake layer. Cake levelers to do the job as well. Don't try to prop an uneven cake with icing. The icing is soft and will give way, causing the cake to become unstable during transport.

Baking Tips and Hints

+ Measure liquids at eye level in standard liquid measuring cups.

+ If using half-round cake pans, position two on a cake circle, add your filling, and then position the next layer with the center crack in the opposite direction for more stability. (see Figure 26)

+ For best results, use large-sized eggs (about ¼ cup each).

+ Time the beating of the cake carefully, beating only for the length of time and at the mixer speed specified in the recipe directions.

+ Premeasure all ingredients so that you can follow the times in your recipe (*mise en place*). You don't want batter to beat longer because you are measuring or looking for an ingredient.

+ Overbeating breaks down the cake structure and causes low volume and shrinkage during the cooling of the cake.

+ Underbeating produces a lumpy batter in which the ingredients are not properly mixed.

+ To determine the amount of batter that a pan holds, measure water in a measuring cup. Pour measured water into the pan. Repeat this process, noting the amount of water used, until the pan is ½ to ⅔ full. Use a ruler to determine the depth.

+ Fill 2" pans ½ full for a 1½" high cake layer, ⅔ full for a 2" high cake layer. 3" deep pans are to be filled only ½ full.

+ Wax or parchment paper, cut to shape, may be used in the bottom of simple geometrically-shaped pans. Do not grease sides, but gently loosen the sides of the cake with a thin spatula after baking.

+ Cool cake in the pan for 10-15 minutes on a cake rack. Larger cakes (over 12" diameter) may need to cool 15 minutes.

+ If a cake has cooled too long and will not release from pan, return it to a warm oven, 250 degrees Fahrenheit, for a few minutes.

+ Character cake pans can be greased and floured or, even easier, sprayed very liberally with a nonstick spray.

+ Un-iced cakes should be stored at room temperature for no more than 24 hours.

+ Bake the cake immediately after mixing. Place as close to the center (both vertical and horizontal center) of the oven as possible. Allow at least an inch of space on all sides and between the pans.

+ You can store cake batter in the refrigerator briefly if you are filling many pans and need to make another batch of cake to fill the oven.

+ Turn on the oven about thirty minutes ahead of time to allow time for it to preheat to the correct baking temperature. You want the interior of the oven to heat, not just the air in the oven.

+ Inaccurate oven temperatures account for a majority of baking problems. Have your oven control checked for accuracy by using a reliable oven thermometer.

+ Preheat the oven and prepare the cake pans before mixing the cake batter so that you can put the cake in the oven immediately.

+ When measuring shortening, fill a two-cup liquid measuring cup with one cup of water. Add the shortening to bring it to the two-cup level. Make sure that all the shortening is submersed. Drain well and empty shortening into the mixing bowl. This is very accurate and the cup is easier to wash.

+ If using more batter than one cake mix yields for a larger pan, mix one package at a time, reduce the oven temperature by about 25 degrees, and increase the baking time.

+ Cake mixes yield about four to six cups of batter. Always measure for accuracy.

+ When filling two pans of the same size, weigh the batter in the pans to ensure equal amounts. A kitchen scale works fine for this.

+ For large cakes, always check for doneness after they have baked for one hour.

+ To remove cake easily from pan, place double thickness paper towel over wire rack. The towel prevents the wire bars from breaking the crust or leaving imprints on top of cake. A clean oven rack or refrigerator shelf can be used for larger layers. Place covered rack over top of cake. Invert cake and rack at least one hour before decorating. Then brush loose crumbs off cake.

+ All 3D pans work best with a firm-textured cake batter (pudding-added mixes and pound cakes). Do not use a traditional white cake, as the crumb is too tender.

+ Be sure pans of a 3D pan set are both greased (with vegetable shortening, not oil or butter) and floured or sprayed with a vegetable spray. Do not grease baking cores.

+ It is important to follow pan directions for batter amounts. Bake cakes on a baking sheet to catch any overflow.

+ Always allow cakes to cool overnight, resting in back half of pan.

+ Use Bake Even Strips for even baking. These easy-to-use strips equalize the baking process by controlling the heat distribution in the pan. The result: moist, level cakes every time without cracked tops or crusty edges and a smooth crust that makes icing and decorating easier.

+ Make your own baking strips by cutting up an old terry cloth towel and wetting it. Wring the towel out. Fold the wet towel and wrap it around the outside of your cake pan. Fasten the end of the towel with a safety pin.

+ Reduce oven temperature 10 to 25 degrees and bake for a longer time for more level cakes.

+ After you've filled your pan with batter, pick up the filled pan and tap it on the countertop a few times. This will help remove excess air bubbles from the batter. Don't tap cakes with whipped eggs, cream, or egg whites, or you'll tap the air out.

+ Spin a cake in a round pan to eliminate air bubbles and allow the cake to bake more evenly.

+ Before torting a cake, mark a small V or notch down the cake side. This will help you align the layers when you put them back together.

+ Use a glaze of apricot jam as a crumb coat. It will seal crumbs and impart an additional light flavor to the cake. Heat the jam and pass through a sieve. Why apricot? It has a less discernable flavor than other fruits.

+ To measure sticky substances like honey or corn syrup, line your measuring cup with plastic wrap, measure your ingredient, gather up the plastic wrap in a pouch, then poke a hole in the bottom to squeeze out the contents. No mess!

+ Use a flower nail, placed flat side down, in a cake pan as a center core to ensure even doneness. Spray the nail well with vegetable oil spray.

+ Baking for too long or at too low of a temperature will result in a dry cake.

+ Use only solid vegetable shortening or spray to grease a nonstick-coating cake pan. Oil and butter will cause the cake to stick and burn.

+ Cut a piece of parchment or wax paper to fit the bottom of the pan, and don't put anything on the sides. When the cake is done, let it sit until you can comfortably touch the cake pan and run a knife around the edges. The cake should come out easily. Don't forget to pull off the parchment paper or waxed paper before icing!

+ Most un-iced, well-wrapped cakes keep in the freezer for up to 6 weeks.

Basic Recipes

Double Vanilla Cake

Ingredients

12 tablespoons unsalted butter, softened
1 cup (200 g) vanilla sugar (see recipe below)
2 cups (250 g) all-purpose flour
2 teaspoons baking powder
¼ teaspoon salt
3 large eggs
¾ cup (175 ml) milk
2 teaspoons vanilla extract

Directions

Yields about 7 cups (1255 g) batter (enough for two 9"x2" cake pans)

Preheat oven to 350° F (175° C). Cut waxed paper or parchment paper circles to fit the bottom of the cake pans.

In a large mixing bowl, beat the butter and vanilla sugar for 5 minutes, until light and fluffy. Stir together flour, baking powder, and salt; and then set aside. Combine the eggs, milk, and vanilla extract.

Add the egg mixture to the butter mixture alternating with the flour mixture, about ⅓ at a time. Scrape the bow often. Beat 2 minutes.

Fill the prepared cake pans halfway. Tap several times gently on the countertop to free any air bubbles. Follow this guide for each pan size, or until a toothpick inserted near the center comes out clean.

Pan Size	Cups of Batter for One Layer	Baking Time
6"	2	25-30 minutes
10"	6	35-40 minutes
14"	10	50-55 minutes

Cake Variations

+ Chocolate Chip - Add 1 ounce (30 g) grated semisweet chocolate to the batter during the last 1 minute of mixing.

+ Lemon Cake - Reduce the milk by 2 tablespoons and add the juice of 1 lemon to the batter, along with the zest of 1 grated lemon. Stir to combine.

+ Italian Cream Cake - Add ½ cup (70 g) finely chopped walnuts or pecans and ½ cup (50 g) shredded coconut to the batter. Stir to combine. Toast the coconut and nuts for a different twist. (Allow to cool before adding to the batter.)

+ Orange Cake - Reduce milk to ¼ cup (60 ml) and add ½ cup (120 ml) orange juice and 1 teaspoon grated orange zest to the batter. Stir to combine.

+ Chocolate Cake – Add 3 tablespoons cocoa.

Vanilla Sugar

Ingredients

One vanilla bean
2 cups (400 g) granulated sugar

Directions

Split the vanilla bean lengthwise and scrape out the seeds with a knife. Put the seeds and bean in a container with the sugar and stir well to combine. Seal the container tightly. The longer the sugar and vanilla sit, the more vanilla flavor will be infused. Keep at room temperature for about a month. Refrigerate for longer life. Use like regular sugar.

Easy Cake

This cake stands up to wedding tortures, including heat and rolled fondant and fills up the pan.

1 cake mix (prefer Duncan Hines)
1 cup water (1¼ cups if chocolate cake mix)

4 serving size "cook and serve" pudding mix, dry
3 eggs
¼ cup vegetable oil
1 envelope whipped topping mix, dry (find in the baking and pudding aisle)

Yields about 7 cups batter (enough for two 9"x2" cake pans)
Preheat oven to 350° F (175° C). Cut waxed paper or parchment paper circles to fit the bottom of the cake pans.

Combine eggs, water, and oil at low speed. Add the dry ingredients and beat at medium speed for 4 minutes. Bake at 350° F (175° C) until a toothpick inserted comes out clean.

Variations
+ Chocolate cake mix, chocolate pudding
+ White cake mix, pistachio pudding
+ Strawberry cake mix, vanilla pudding
+ Lemon cake mix, lemon pudding

Fresh Strawberry Filling

Ingredients
1 lb (460 g) strawberries, hulled and chopped
½ cup (100 g) vanilla sugar (see recipe from *Double Vanilla Cake*)
2½ tablespoons cornstarch
½ teaspoon amaretto or almond extract, optional

Directions
In a heavy small sauce pan combine the strawberries, sugar, and cornstarch. Stir constantly and crush berries slightly with back of spoon or potato masher. Boil 2 minutes to thicken, stirring constantly (mixture will be slightly chunky). Pour into bowl and cool completely. Stir in the amaretto or almond extract, if desired. Yields 2 cups.

The Icing On the Cake

Icing is the Foundation

The icing on the cake is the foundation that your decorations will enhance. You need to practice icing cakes and developing your technique in getting the sides smooth and perfect. There are numerous tools for smoothing cake icing – spatulas, scrapers, paper towels, hot water, and a turntable. The best tool is the icing consistency. The icing needs to be thin enough not to pull crumbs from the cake. Thin it with water or the liquid used in the recipe to make it the right consistency.

Icing Tips & Hints

+ Thin buttercream icing with milk or light corn syrup to thin consistency. Cream adds a nice piping consistency and a tasty icing.

+ Adding confectioners' sugar and mixing well will stiffen consistency.

+ When icing cakes smooth, the consistency is correct when the spatula glides over the icing smoothly.

+ Buttercream icing can be refrigerated in an airtight container for two weeks.

+ Buttercream icing can also be frozen in an airtight container for up to three months. Let the frozen icing come to room temperature and re-beat on medium speed to restore its consistency.

+ Use a few drops of orange and lemon extract in your icing to add a pleasant taste. It's not overwhelmingly citrus, but will round out the flavor.

+ Mix piping gel into icing for writing and making leaves. It's shinier and the leaves pull out to nice points.

+ Crumb coating is a thin layer of medium consistency icing which causes crumbs to adhere to the cake so that they won't be visible in the final icing layer. Crumb coating can be thinned icing, piping gel, or melted and strained apricot preserves.

+ If you find it difficult to obtain a smooth icing on your cake, use a decorator's comb to give the icing an interesting texture.

+ Bulging cakes? Don't use so much filling! Use a dense or thick consistency filling and be sparing. When the top layers press down (thanks to gravity) the filling can only squeeze out the sides and cause a bulge. Instead of two layers of cake with one layer of filling, torte the cakes so that you have multiple layers of filling. You will taste the filling and not use as much.

+ Another solution for bulging cake sides is to ice the cake with a crumb coat, then let it set overnight. This will allow the cake to settle.

+ Pipe an icing dam around the edge of each layer to contain the filling, especially if the filling is a different color than the icing on the cake. Use a #10, #11, or #12 round tip or cut the end of your parchment bag to pipe the dam which will keep the filling from squeezing out the sides.

+ Air bubbles on the iced cake? If the cake is cold when it is iced, you may get air bubbles or pockets in your icing because your cake is breathing. No problem! Poke a tiny hole in the bubble with a pin or toothpick and gently smooth the bubble down with your hand.

+ Stiffen too-thin royal icing with cornstarch.

+ Use a stiff straightedge to smooth the sides of a cake. Hold the straightedge stationary and spin the turntable.

+ Smooth buttercream icing on a cake with a paper towel. Use a buttercream that 'crusts' or is dry to the touch after about 15 to 30 minutes. Use a paper towel that has no designs for a perfectly smooth cake or one with quilted designs for a fun cake. Lay the towel over the cake and rub lightly with the palm of your hand or a fondant smoother. Don't use your fingers. If the paper towel sticks to the icing, it needs more time to dry.

+ If a crust has formed on top of your icing in the bowl, don't stir it up or you will have pieces of sugar that will clog tips and be gritty on your iced cake. Carefully scrape off the hard layer and stir until the buttercream is spreadable again. Keep the bowl covered to prevent drying out.

+ Use an 18" decorating bag and tip #789 to ice any size or shape cake. Smooth the sides with a spatula or scraper with a straightedge.

+ Put wax paper strips under the edges of your cake. Ice the cake as normal. Gently pull out the strips and the cake plate will remain clean.

+ A hot (not wet) spatula can be used to smooth out icing. Keep a towel and a tall glass of hot water near and dip the spatula to clean and heat it before each stroke.

+ A piece of rubberized shelf liner will keep your cake board from slipping on your turntable as you ice and decorate.

+ For a quick drizzled icing, heat canned chocolate icing in the microwave until just pourable. Drizzle on the cake with a fork or a decorating bag, cut slightly open.

+ To keep royal icing from setting up, add a small amount of glycerin.

+ Corn syrup added to a boiling sugar solution will prevent the sugar from crystallizing.

+ To be sure your bowl is clean for royal icing, scrub the inside with dry table salt and a paper towel. Discard the salt and wipe the bowl with a clean paper towel.

Basic Recipes

Buttercream with Cream Cheese

Ingredients
Dash of salt
⅓ (80 ml) cup milk
3½ oz (100 g) cream cheese, not fat free
1 cup (150 g) shortening, white or butter flavor, or high ratio
1 teaspoon vanilla extract
¼ teaspoon lemon extract
¼ teaspoon orange extract
2 lbs (915 g) confectioner's sugar (also called icing sugar)

Directions
Dissolve the salt in the milk. Beat cream cheese with the shortening until smooth. Combine milk/salt mixture with extracts. Add milk/salt mixture slowly to cream cheese on low speed. Mix until smooth. Add the sugar a little at a time until mixed. Continue to mix until smooth on low speed. Yields 3 cups.

Cream Cheese Icing

This recipe makes a great icing and filling for carrot or Italian cream cakes.

Ingredients
16 oz (454 g) cream cheese, not fat free, not softened
2 lbs (915 g) confectioner's sugar (also called icing sugar)
2 sticks of butter, room temperature
1 teaspoon vanilla
2 tablespoons milk, half & half, cream, or orange juice

Directions

Combine cream cheese, butter, vanilla, and milk. Beat in confectioner's sugar until smooth and creamy. Yields 3 cups.

Ganache

Ganache can be used as a glaze, whipped for an icing and filling, or solid for truffles. You can use dark, milk, or white chocolate, but be sure to use a high-quality chocolate for the best taste and results.

Ingredients

8 ounces (227 g) good quality chocolate, by weight, chopped
8 ounces (227 g) heavy whipping cream, by weight
Liqueur, optional, 1-2 teaspoons

Directions

Place the chocolate in a medium-sized glass or stainless steel bowl. Set aside.

Heat the cream in a medium-sized saucepan over medium heat, bringing just to a boil. Pour the boiling cream over the chocolate and allow it to stand for a few minutes.

Stir with a whisk until smooth. If desired, add the liqueur to taste.

Basic Buttercream Icing

Ingredients

2 lbs (915 g) confectioner's sugar (also called icing sugar)
2 sticks of butter
2 teaspoons high-quality vanilla
3 tablespoons milk, half & half, or cream

Directions

Beat butter until creamy and white in color. Add vanilla and milk. Add confectioner's sugar and beat at low speed until creamy and smooth.

If too thick to spread, add milk by the teaspoon until the desired consistency. If too thin, add confectioner's sugar a little bit at a time. Yields 4-5 cups.

My First Icing

I learned how to make this icing when I was starting out. It's tasty, not too sweet, and holds up in humid, hot climates. (I grew up in Florida).

Ingredients
1½ cups shortening
1 envelope dry whipped topping (find in the baking and pudding aisle)
1 teaspoon vanilla
½ teaspoon orange extract
½ teaspoon lemon extract
½ cup all-purpose, white flour
¾ cup milk, half & half, or cream
2 lbs (915 g) confectioners' sugar (also called icing sugar)
Pinch of salt, dissolved in milk

Directions
Beat together shortening, powdered whipped topping, and flavorings until stiff. Add milk and beat until creamy. Add flower and combine. Add confectioner's sugar and beat at low speed until creamy and smooth. Yields 3 cups (690 g).

Transporting the Cake

Moving a tiered cake from one location to another does not have to be difficult. In actuality, it can be quite easy! Following some simple guidelines ensures that your cake will arrive safely—whether you are traveling hundreds of miles or just a few.

> # Plan ahead!!!
> ## Allow plenty of travel time and know where you are going.

Place the cakes in clean, covered, sturdy boxes that are sized to the baseboard of each cake. This will prevent the cake from shifting within the box and possibly crushing the sides of the cake. If the box is too big, or the cake board is the same size as the cake, roll pieces of masking tape sticky side out and attach to the inside bottom of the box or use rubberized shelf liner to keep the cake from sliding. Position the cake base on top of the tape or shelf liner. For boxes which must hold taller decorations, prop up top and sides and secure with tape. Cover lightly with plastic wrap to keep out dust.

Use a corrugated cardboard box the same size as your cake base to transport stacked cakes and large cakes. Tape the box like you would if you were packing an item for shipment, but don't close the top. Cut down two adjacent sides to form a fold-down flap. Slide your cake in and tale the sides, making a small tab to easily pull the tape and box open. (see Figure 27)

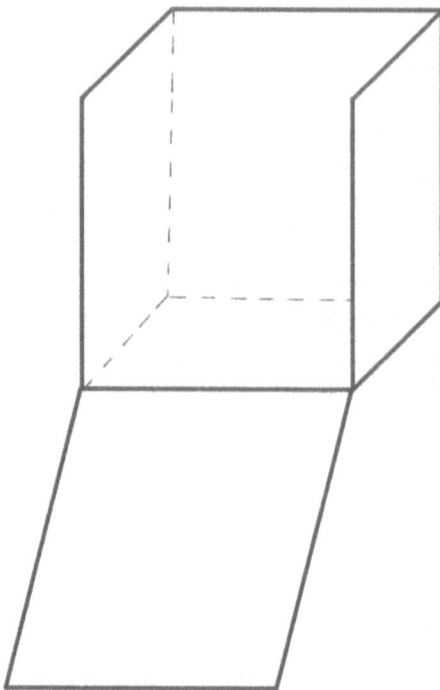

Figure 27 – Cut the box down the front corners for east of inserting the cake

I have always lived in hot climates, first in Florida, and now in Central Texas. You haven't lived until you've delivered a wedding cake in a humid, 105-degree temperature. For this reason, I refrigerate my cakes for several hours or overnight (boxed and ready to go), then load them into my SUV, pre-cooled by running the air conditioner. This way, I stand a good chance that I will deliver a cake in one piece. Here are some other tips for making the delivery smooth:

Tips for Smooth Deliveries

+ Use a nonskid rubber mat carpet foam pad to protect cakes. Rubberized shelf liner works well and is very economical.

+ You may want to consider a "Cake in Delivery" or "Cake on Board" sign. Print one on the computer and cover it with clear contact paper to make it sturdy. If nothing else, it will explain to the drivers behind you why you are going so slow and they might not honk as much.

+ If it's hot and you do not have a refrigerated SUV or van, keep the cake away from or cover the windows. Transport a cold (refrigerated) cake, turn your vehicle's air conditioning on before loading, and use insulated boxes if available.

+ A large insulated box or cover can be made by duct-taping or gluing together sheets of foil-backed insulation foam from the hardware store.

+ For tiers the same size as the separator plates, cut dowels to 3" length. Place one plate upside down, insert dowels, and place the cake and plate on the dowels. This also works well to decorate the tier. Use crystal twist cake plates for this tip.

Cakes on Pillars

Transport the cakes separately and assemble at the reception site. Toppers, candles, and ornaments should be removed from cakes when they are being moved. Pack these items separately and transport them away from the cake to avoid damage.

Stacked Cakes

Depending on the size of the cake, you can move the entire cake. For a larger number of tiers, transport unassembled and assemble at the reception. Be sure to take the equipment and icings you will need to finish any decorating needed after assembly at the reception.

Many times the location of the reception – up a hill, over a dirt road, or a journey of many hours away – will determine how you transport the cake. ALWAYS be conservative. Don't cut corners or you could be repairing your cake upon arrival.

The weight of a cake is key. Determine how much you or your assistant can lift and keep each tier manageable. Remember that rolled fondant adds quite a bit of weight.

Center Column Construction

Take tiers apart if constructed in Center Column method. Position the plates on rubberized shelf liner resting in a cake pan.

At the Reception Site

Scout out the site before you carry anything in. If possible, take someone with you so that she can stay in the car with the cake; and leave on the air conditioning if it's hot outside.

Take a cart or, at the destination, request a cart on wheels to move the cake into the reception area. This is easier and safer than carrying by hand. A collapsible delivery cart can come in handy, especially when you have many layers to deliver, one very heavy layer, or a long way to walk. You can find one at office or restaurant supply stores or on the internet. Uline has a nice one for under $100. (See the Resource section.)

Remove the cakes from the boxes on the reception table by cutting the sides of the boxes and sliding the cakes out. Bring along a repair kit—extra icing, prepared decorating bags and tips, flowers, spatulas—just in case it is necessary to make any repairs. Enlist the help of someone at the site. There's usually someone on the staff who will help.

Check the table for levelness and stability before you set the cake on it. Lean on the edge to see if it tilts. Use your level if you are not sure.

Delivery kit

Take a delivery kit with you to fix any problems that may arise when you deliver the cake. The following checklist is more comprehensive than you will need, but it serves as a guide to build your own list.

- ☐ A congratulations card for the wedding couple
- ☐ Apron (great advertising of you have your company name on it)
- ☐ Small adhesive bandages (just in case)
- ☐ Box for top tier cake
- ☐ Box or bag for plates and columns to be returned
- ☐ Business cards (Note: There are always brides and grooms, and families, scouting out venues when you are setting up.)
- ☐ Cake top ornament, initials, flowers
- ☐ Camera and extra batteries
- ☐ Clean Styrofoam meat tray or plastic lid (to place flowers on top so that they don't touch the cake)
- ☐ Columns/pillars, plus extras
- ☐ Contract / invoice / delivery form
- ☐ Cutting/serving instructions (See Appendix I for an example.)

- ☐ Decorating bags of the icing colors used and tips
- ☐ Doorstop
- ☐ Florist tape
- ☐ Florist wire
- ☐ Flower spikes
- ☐ Fresh or silk flowers and greenery
- ☐ Extra icing flowers
- ☐ Food service gloves
- ☐ Level
- ☐ List of pieces to be returned
- ☐ Map to reception/party site
- ☐ Matches or lighter (to light candles for photos)
- ☐ Measuring tape
- ☐ Moist washcloth in plastic bag or moist wipes
- ☐ Skewers
- ☐ Oasis (florist foam)
- ☐ Paper towels
- ☐ Pen and pencil
- ☐ Picture or sketch of the cake
- ☐ Ribbon
- ☐ Scissors that can also cut wire and flower stems
- ☐ Shims or matchbooks to correct uneven tables
- ☐ Small garbage bag
- ☐ Small hot-glue gun and glue sticks
- ☐ Spatulas
- ☐ Stairways & bridges necessary for design
- ☐ Straight or safety pins (for securing fabric when necessary)
- ☐ Tape (transparent) and double-sided tape
- ☐ Telephone number of contact person – get a cell number
- ☐ Telephone number of site
- ☐ Toothpicks
- ☐ Tulle (in case the table needs help)
- ☐ Wax or parchment paper

Fountain Items

- ☐ Cascade set
- ☐ Color for water
- ☐ Distilled water

- ☐ Duct tape
- ☐ Extension cords (mark with your name and phone number)
- ☐ Flower Holder Ring
- ☐ Fountain (check for proper operation before event and provide a box for safe return)

Running a Cake Business

References

Your business is your reputation. A good reputation can go a long way to help you gain more business, but a bad reputation will spread even faster.

Each experience you have with customers in your business has one of three results that affect your reputation:

The first result stems from an experience you have with a customer, or potential customer, where you don't do anything really wrong, but you also don't stand out from anyone else. This may not seem like the most harmful result, but it is close. At best, you will be considered standard in the mind of a customer. The customer will probably forget you; but if she does remember you, she'll consider you as someone who was average last time.

The second result occurs when you, or your worker, has erred badly enough to make the customer really mad at you. The worst has just happened for your business. Besides losing a customer, you have also lost anyone who happens to talk with that person about your business. There is no way to calculate the full damage that will result from this. If you, as a business owner, allow this to happen, then you certainly deserve the impact it has on your business. However, nine times out of ten, the business owner is unaware of what has happened if the problem occurred with one of her employees, or even out of her own interactions with the customer. Don't assume that dissatisfied people will make the effort to let you know what happened. Usually they just don't come back and you have no way to remedy it. If you uncover the problem, but neglect to fix it, then you deserve the bad press you receive. However, if you take the initiative to go above and beyond to correct the problem, you will prove to the customer that you so value her loyalty that you will go the any length to satisfy her and make it right.

Result number three is what all business owners should seek in all interactions they have with others. You aim to make your customers, and potential customers, believe that, in addition to furnishing high-quality services or materials, you are devoted to how well services or materials satisfy customer needs. You are focused on forming a lasting bond with your customers so that they know you are committed to filling their needs. When you achieve this goal, you can trust that you've won a loyal customer whose value far surpasses any purchase she may make today (Menzies).

When you have these good experiences with a customer, ask if she will serve as a reference. Ask her to write a sentence or two about her experience and whether you can post these testimonials on your website. You should also include thank you cards and notes in your portfolio or frame them for your office where you meet with potential customers.

Advertising

Business Cards

You can find nice cardstock business card forms in the local office supply store or on the internet to print your own custom business cards. You could probably barter a cake with your local printer for business cards as well. Check the *Resources* section for information.

Cakes Donated to Events and Charities

Churches, schools, nursing homes, animal shelters, and other organizations always need cakes or cupcakes, but seldom have the funds to buy them. Provide the baked goods in exchange for your business cards placed in a prominent location on the goodie table.

Stationery

You can buy stationery to match your business cards or make it easily on your computer. Your business name, your name, phone number, email address or website address looks nice at the top of your letterhead for thank you notes or other business correspondence.

Brochures

Brochure paper is also available at your local office supply store to match your business cards and stationery. The printing instructions are on the paper and work with most current word processing software applications.

Use Press Releases

Send a press release to local and nearby newspapers every time you participate in nonprofit or community events in your town. You should also send a press release if you have anything happen with your business. When you do, be sure to mention everything that makes your business unique. This will be a bit of advertisement along with the announcement.

Advertise in Local Newspapers or Shoppers

Use your advertising budget wisely and run ads in papers where you will benefit. Start with small shopper papers, bulletin boards, or college papers. Offer a special and be sure to include the end date or you will have people coming to you after the offer has ended.

Partner with Other Wedding Businesses

Whenever you deliver a wedding cake, meet the venue manager or owner and talk with her a few minutes. Exchange business cards and ask for and offer referrals. You can also exchange cards with wedding planners, florists, photographers, caterers, DJs, and all the people related to the wedding. This will give you a good portfolio of contacts and referrals for brides. You can even trade services, including professional photographs of your cakes.

Real Estate Offices

Work with a real estate office to provide a cake to new homeowners in the area. The cake should be in a nice box with your business information printed on it or on an attached label.

Health Regulations and Legal Considerations

If your business has grown enough for you to know that you must approach this as a real business (instead of a money making hobby), these are the things you should do. Check with your local health department for the requirements for operating a legal, health- inspected food facility in your town. Each state and town has different requirements. Some states are very lenient with small home baking businesses and only require you to get legal when you surpass their limits. Other states or cities just pretend you aren't really there. If you happen to be in a city with a very strict health department, you must comply or risk being fined (Moore, Earlene Moore's Web Site).

Cottage Food Laws

At least fourteen states have a home baker's or cottage food law which allows nonperishable baked goods to be made and sold from the home. States that have a cottage food law as of this writing are Iowa, Maine, Massachusetts, New Hampshire, New Mexico, North Carolina, Ohio (Ohio Cottage Foods Statute), Oregon, Pennsylvania, Tennessee, Utah, Vermont, Virginia, and Wyoming. Alabama and Indiana allow home baking for the purpose of selling at a Farmer's Market. Several states either have a law in progress or have tried to pass a law in recent years including: Texas, Oklahoma, New Jersey, Maryland, Michigan, and Florida. If you have an interest in supporting a law for your state, visit the web site for the Texas Cottage Food Law at www.texascottagefoodlaw.com.

Tracking Orders and Figuring Costs

Most people don't charge enough for their work.

You need to figure out how much your ingredients cost and what your time is worth in order to price your cakes correctly, because you will be surprised how much work you put into the cake and how much the ingredients cost compared to your pricing. A good rule of thumb is to charge three times the cost of your ingredients. This is an estimate only, to show you that quality cakes cost money to create. Don't compare yourself to the local grocery store bakery, which may not even bake their own cakes. (They may have them shipped in already baked and weeks old.) These bakeries work on volume and low profit margins.

If you have even just minimal computer skills, I recommend a software called CakeBoss by Masters Software (see Resources section). CakeBoss (no relation to the TLC television show) takes your local facts, such as cost of ingredients, labor, etc. and helps you figure out how much to charge. It also tracks quotes and orders, making your taxes much easier. Here's what CakeBoss can do for you...

+ Calculate the exact cost of a cake, including your hourly labor. Never again wonder how much to charge.
+ Keep track of customer data and orders with both spreadsheets and an at-a-glance planning calendar
+ Cost out recipes easily
+ Print shopping lists for orders
+ Calculate profit for each order
+ Track all expenses
+ Attach photos to orders
+ Print customer invoices with your own business logo.
+ Run reports to show you exactly where your revenue is coming from.
+ Get organized - never lose an order or phone number again! This is handy for sending an anniversary card to the bride and groom. Many cakes I do are anniversaries, christenings, and birthdays – all from that one wedding cake.

Bibliography

Armstrong, Karen. *Cake Frosting: Cake Frosting Recipes, Wedding Cake Frosting, Cake Decoration and More*. Createspace, 2010.

Brown, Debbie. *Debbie Brown's Dream Wedding Cakes: Gorgeous Designs for Weddings, Anniversaries and Other Romantic Occasions*. B.Dutton Publishing (A Division of Squires Kitchen Magazine Publishing Ltd.), 2008.

Charsley, Simon R. *Wedding Cakes and Cultural History*. Routledge, 1992.

Clark, Beverly. *Beverly Clark's Book of Wedding Cakes*. Running Press Book Publishers, 1999.

Clark, Beverly. *Weddings: A Celebration*. Beverly Clark Collection, 1996.

Coward, Sylvia. *Wedding Cakes: Exciting Designs with Full Step-By-Step Instructions*. Sterling Publishing, 1995.

Dunn, Alan. *Floral Wedding Cakes & Sprays*. Merehurst Ltd, 1999.

Dunn, Alan. *Flowers and Foliage for Wedding Cakes*. B.Dutton Publishing (A Division of Squires Kitchen Magazine Publishing Ltd.), 2005.

Dunn, Alan. *The Wedding Cake Decorator's Bible: A Resource of Mix-and-Match Designs and Embellishments*. David & Charles, 2009.

Ford, Mary. *Wedding Cakes (Classic Step-by-Step)*. Michael O'Mara Books, 1994

Gage, Fran. *A Sweet Quartet: Sugar, Almonds, Eggs, and Butter: A Baker's Tour, Including 33 Recipes*. North Point Press, 2003

Garrett, Toba M. *Wedding Cake Art and Design: A Professional Approach*. Wiley, 2010.

Goble, Karen. *Quick & Easy Wedding Cakes*. New Holland, 2006

Hackett, Kathleen. *Wedding Cakes*. Hearst Books, 2003. *paperback, 2006.*

Herbert, Lesley. *Ultimate Book of Wedding Cakes*. Merehurst Ltd, 1994.

Howlett, Lorraine Sorby , Marien Jones (Contributor). *Cake Decorating Wedding Designs*. Merehurst, 1987.

Hurst, Nadene, Julie Springall. *Contemporary Wedding Cakes*. Charles E. Tuttle Co, 2000.

Johnson, Klara. *Wedding Cakes*. K&N Marketing Associates, 1993.

Latour, Shalini. *The Icing On The Cake: Fabulous Decorating Ideas for Simply Stylish Cakes*. North Light Books, 2004

MacGregor, Elaine. *Wedding Cakes from Start to Finish*. Souvenir Pr Ltd, 1994.

MacGregor, Elaine. *Wedding Cakes*. Slawson Communications, 1988.

Manchester, Kate, Sylvia Weinstock. *The Perfect Wedding Cake*. Stewart, Tabori & Chang, 2001.

Matthews, Bette. *Cakes (For Your Wedding)*. Friedman/Fairfax Publishing, 2001.

McCann, Dolores. *A Workbook of Wedding Cakes*. Sugarcraft, 2003.

Murphy, Esther, Del Carnes (Editor). *Mrs Mayo's How to Make a Wedding Cake*. Deco Pr Pub Co, 1992.

Pawsey, Linda. *New Wedding Cake Designs*. Merehurst Ltd, 2000.

Peters, Colette. *Colette's Wedding Cakes*. Little Brown & Company, 1997.

Roney, Carley. *The Knot Ultimate Wedding Lookbook: More Than 1,000 Cakes, Centerpieces, Bouquets, Dresses, Decorations, and Ideas for the Perfect Day*. Clarkson Potter, 2010.

Shaffer, Lynda. *Wedding Flowers and Decorations Ideas Books on CD (12 Flower books with 1000 Wedding Bouquets, Cakes, Centerpieces, Arrangements, Floral Wedding Planner & More) (CD-ROM)*. Shaffer & Shaffer Ltd., 2005.

Slattery, John. *Chocolate Cakes for Weddings and Celebrations*. Merehurst Ltd, 2002.

Stewart, Martha. *Weddings*. Clarkson N. Potter, Inc., 1987.

Stewart, Martha. *The Best of Martha Stewart Living Weddings*. Clarkson Potter, 1999.

Stewart, Martha and Kromer, Wendy. *Martha Stewart's Wedding Cakes*. Clarkson Potter, 2007.

Sullivan, Eugene T. and Sullivan, Marilynn C. *The Wilton Book of Wedding Cakes*. Wilton Enterprises, 1971.

Sullivan, Eugene T. and Sullivan, Marilynn C. *Wilton Shows You How to Create Dramatic Tier Cakes*. Wilton Enterprises, 1985.

Sullivan, Marilynn C. (Editor). *Celebrate! Wedding Cakes*. Wilton Enterprises, 1983.

Turner, Mitch. *Wedding Cakes*. Universe, 2009.

Turner, Mitch. *Couture Wedding Cakes*. Jacqui Small LLP, 2009.

Vincent, Kerry. *Romantic Wedding Cakes*. Merehurst Ltd, 2001.

Way, Beverley. *Wedding Cakes: The Beverley Way Collection (Volume 1)*. BookSurge Publishing, 2009.

Wilson, Dede. *The Wedding Cake Book*. John Wiley & Sons, 1997.

Wilson, Dede. *Wedding Cakes You Can Make: Designing, Baking, and Decorating the Perfect Wedding Cake*. John Wiley & Sons, 2005.

Wilton Enterprises. *A Treasury of Wilton Wedding Cakes*. Wilton Enterprises, 1991.

Wilton Enterprises. *Wedding Cakes: A Wilton Album*. Wilton Enterprises, 1989.

Wilton Enterprises. *Wilton Bridal Cakes: A Wilton Album*. Wilton Enterprises, 1993.

Wilton Enterprises. *Wilton Tiered Cakes*. Wilton Enterprises, 2006

Wilton Enterprises. *Wilton Wedding Cakes – A Romantic Portfolio*. Wilton Enterprises, 2000.

Wilton Enterprises. *Wilton Wedding Dream Cakes*. Wilton Enterprises, 2000.

Wilton Enterprises. *Wilton Weddings*. Wilton Enterprises, 1996.

Web Sites

These web sites have information about wedding cakes, including lots of pictures. Use any popular search engine to find many more. Find your favorite decorator and business on Facebook, Twitter, LinkedIn, and YouTube as well.

American Cake Decorator – www.americancakedecorating.com - Whether you are an experienced sugar artist or just learning to decorate, American Cake Decorating is your source for techniques, tips, and news.

Baking 911 - www.baking911.com - Gain access to over 2,000 professional and tested recipes, many with step-by-step instructional tutorials and color photos. Become a part of an active 60,000 member baking community. Ask, learn, and discuss. Post your own recipes.

Bride's Magazine – www.brides.com – Stay current on the latest wedding cake trends in the industry.

Cake Central – www.cakecentral.com - If you're a beginner or a professional cake decorator... here you can share recipes, talk with other cake decorators, find new cake decorating ideas in our cake photo galleries, and all for free!

Colette Peter's Web Site – www.colettescakes.com – Beautiful cakes to inspire you.

eWedding Cake - www.eweddingcake.com - This is the complete portal for all information you will need on wedding cakes. Here are many different designs, types, colors, flavors, designer, prices and shapes of wedding cakes to choose from. The best way to choose what you like is to look at pictures of cakes.

International Cake Exploration Societé (ICES) – www.ices.org – Welcome to the International Cake Exploration Societé (ICES), an organization comprised of over 4000 sugar artists, cake decorators and vendors from all over the world. Our sugar art masterpieces can be as small as one exquisite gum paste rose or as large as the beautiful towering sugar sculptures you've seen on televised competitions. Whether you'd like to learn more about the sugar art craft, or if you've been teaching cake decorating for years, ICES has a place just for you.

The Knot – www.theknot.com – The definitive site for brides planning their weddings. Check this site out for great ideas on the latest wedding cake trends.

Martha Stewart – www.marthastewartweddings.com – Inspiration from the top cake designers. If it's on Martha's site, brides will want it.

PastryWiz - www.pastrywiz.com/wedding - On these pages you will find a mixture of wedding cake history, basic and advanced cake decorating recipes, as well as a variety of wedding resources.

Ron Ben Israel Cakes – www.weddingcakes.com – Amazing cakes from the master artist, Ron Ben Israel.

Super Weddings - www.superweddings.com/cakegallery.htm - The SuperWeddngs.com Wedding Cakes Photo Gallery features a collection of wedding cakes that have been hand-picked for exquisite design by our editor, Linda Kevich. Each cake in the Gallery is a masterpiece of creativity and talent. An internationally recognized wedding expert with nearly 20 years experience, Ms. Kevich has seen thousands of cakes during her career; the designs you will find here are truly among the best of the best...

Wedding Channel – www.weddingchannel.com - 100,000+ wedding photographers, florists, and more -- rated by brides!

Wikipedia - http://en.wikipedia.org/wiki/Wedding_cake - Information about the history and traditions of wedding and groom's cakes.

Resources

Cake Decorating Supplies

Advantage Bridal - www.advantagebridal.com - Your wedding cake topper will be one thing that everyone in attendance will notice, whether it is a comical cake topper or a very formal Swarovski crystal monogram cake topper. Monogram cake toppers are all the rage and we have the largest online selection right here! Swarovski crystal monogram cake toppers are extremely popular, and best of all, you can frame your monogram cake jewelry and enjoy it in your home long after the wedding is over.

All in One Bake Shop - www.allinonebakeshop.com - the retail supply source for baking supplies, products and accessories for home and professional bakers and decorators, with products available locally in our store or across the country by mail order

Bakels - www.bakels.com - Bakels manufacture and distribute a wide range of quality ingredients tailor made for the bakery, confectionery and foodservice sectors.

Beryls - www.beryls.com - Beryl's Cake Decorating & Pastry Supplies Let us be your confection connection for imported British & European Cake Decorating & Pastry Supplies - Fine Quality and Friendly Service. THE WORLD OF DECORATING AT YOUR FINGER TIPS!

Cake Craft Shoppe - www.cakecraftshoppe.com - Currently one of the largest importers of English products used predominantly for Fondant and Gum Paste. Not only do they sell the products over the Internet, but also at events such as Days-of-Sharing, Cake Shows, and the ICES Conventions. In addition to selling top quality cake decorating supplies, Cake Craft Shoppe offers a large classroom where basic through advanced cake decorating classes are taught. They provide a number of guest instructor classes each year that are taught by top sugar artists from around the world!

Cake Stands - www.cakestands.com – Home of the asymmetrical cake stand. This patented wedding cake stand that is rock solid, incredibly versatile, and easy to assemble. In this revolutionary new design, the legs are actually attached to the plates with screws. This design provides the security and stability cake decorating professionals require. It's ingenious two plate system allows for the application of bottom borders prior to setup, which will save countless hours of setup time. The stand can be set up in an amazing variety of levels and designs.

Country Kitchen Sweet Art - www.countrykitchensa.com – Country Kitchen Sweet Art - Country Kitchen SweetArt is a family-owned business that has been around for over 45 years. We have a passion for the confectionary arts and have chosen cake decorating supplies, candy making supplies and kitchen and baking supplies and tools that we use and enjoy. We have grown from a small business to over 14,000 square feet of sales area in Fort Wayne, Indiana. Our business caters to walk-in store sales, catalog sales, and our online store.

Dallas Foam – www.dallas-foam.com – Great selection of Styrofoam cake dummies at good prices. Custom work also.

Designer Stencils - www.designerstencils.com - Designer Stencils, a family owned business since 1982, is the company that meets all the needs of the customer. We design, cut, and package all of our stencils, which gives us the flexibility of custom designs, size changes, and plastic modifications. You'll be able to find the right stencil you are looking for, such as: art deco, architectural designs, country, culinary, seashore, jungle, lettering, and much more to help you decorate your home or business.

Lucks - www.lucks.com - Lucks Food Decorating Company is committed to providing the baking industry with quality edible products to enhance decorators' creativity. As the leading manufacturer of edible food decorations for cakes and confections, we offer innovative, time-saving products, including Edible Image® designs, Dec-Ons® molded sugar decorations, Print-Ons® Sheets, Designer Prints™ decorations, Royal Icing Roses and Colors. All of Lucks manufactured products are USA-made in FDA inspected and registered facilities. Look to us as your creative resource for tips, products, ideas and food decorating solutions. Lucks is the innovator of Edible Images™ brand decorations.

Nicholas Lodge – www.nicholaslodge.com - The International Sugar Art Collection School of Sugar Art, teaches all levels and aspects of sugar art and cake decorating. The International Sugar Art Collection, is the division that manufactures and distributes over 400 specialized tools and equipment use in creating sugar art and cakes. The school, offices, retail gallery, and product distribution are located in Norcross, Georgia, just a few miles north of downtown Atlanta, which has been home for Nicholas since 1991.

Stress Free Cake Supports – www.stressfreecakes.com - Stress Free Cake Supports were developed to help cake decorators build a solid, stable cake. The Stress Free Cake Supports are a set of stainless steel discs with threaded bolts welded on the disc. NSF Delrin® legs are threaded onto the bolts forming a solid support to use while stacking your cake. This design has revolutionized stacked cakes.

Sugarcraft - www.sugarcraft.com - over 30,000 cake, candy, cookie, pie, baking products - Wholesale and Retail Worldwide - Get it all in one place and save shipping costs! We supply hard-to-find baking tools, ingredients, and supplies for creative decorators around the world.

Sunflower Sugar Art - www.sunflowersugarartusa.com - Company founder and CEO Pilar Gonzalez has conceived, designed, and refined the details of virtually everything we produce. For 20 years now, she has guided Sunflower Sugar Art USA as an innovator in the world of sugar craft. We remain committed to helping you design top-quality cakes and sugar craft items by providing you with top-quality silicone molds, metal cutters, craft colors and sugar-working tools.

Wedding Cake Stands - www.weddingcakestand.net - Browse the great selection of wedding cake stands from the popular new Cupcake Tree Stand and the elegant Silver Cake Base to the unique Cascading Cake Stands and Scroll Garden Stands. We have something for everyone, all at convenient and secure online shopping.

Wedding Cake Stands - www.weddingcakestands.com - His Designs' cake stands and cake plateaus are creative, sturdy and affordable. We design and manufacture our own acrylic cake stands. We buy our plateaus direct from the manufacturer giving you a lower price. Compared to other plateaus:

Our plating and finish are of a higher quality. Our larger round plateaus have extra legs for more strength and support.

Wedding Cake Stands - www.wedding-cake-stands.com - Do you stress stacking cakes? Tired of cutting dowels? Want to know how to make a wedding cake straight and perfect every time? Is there a tiered cake stand stacking system that can hold a wedding cake of any size secure during transport? The Cake Stackers™ tiered wedding cake stand is the most secure; time saving and cost effective cake support system available.

Wilton - www.wilton.com - Wilton helps families celebrate! For 80 years, Wilton has been the industry leader in cake decorating, quality bakeware, and food crafting. We are the number one resource for nationally-located decorating classes, proven supplier of professional Wilton decorating bakeware, and provide step-by-step information online and thru our publications to help you make your celebration special with Wilton cakes, cookies, cupcakes and candy.

Winbeckler - www.winbeckler.com – Home to the Winbeckler's website – a collection of supplies, books, and teaching.

WMI Designs – www.wmidesigns.com – Beautiful initials and wording for wedding cakes. Includes Monogram Cake Toppers, Partially Decorated Toppers, Fully Decorated Toppers, Cake Pick Cake Toppers, Word Cake Toppers, Shape Cake Toppers, Keepsake Display Boxes, Swarovski Crystals, Wedding Car Decorations, Church Decorations, and Wedding Picture Frames

Photo Sharing

Flickr - www.flickr.com - Flickr was the first such site to recognize itself as much more than a hosting service for personal photo albums.

Seehere - www.seehere.com – Photo sharing, plus prints, books, mugs, clothes, posters, cards, and gifts with your photos.

Shutterfly - www.shutterfly.com - Shutterfly attempts to differentiate itself from other online photo services by allowing unlimited images at no cost.

The service also keeps uploaded photos are their full resolution, rather than scaling down images or otherwise affecting the originals.

Photo Books

Kodak Gallery - www.kodakgallery.com/photo-books - From creation to completion—it's all about delivering a beautiful finished product of outstanding KODAK quality to you, now faster than ever.

Lulu - www.lulu.com/publish/photo_books - Create photo books, custom photobooks, photo album books, digital photo books, photobooks for yourself or to sell

My Publisher - www.mypublisher.com - Turn digital photos into cards, calendars, and coffee table books with My Publisher. A memorable, high-quality gift.

Photoworks - www.photoworks.com - Create personalized photo books, photo cards, custom calendars, and photo gifts from your digital pictures. Share your images online for free.

Seehere - www.seehere.com - Design your own photo book or have it created for you automatically.

Shutterfly - www.shutterfly.com/photo-books - Shutterfly's photo books are a beautiful and long-lasting way to print and preserve your favorite digital photo memories.

SmileBooks - www.smilebooks.com - Stunning Photo Books that are easy to build. Preserve your priceless memories for generations to come in a SmileBooks Photo Book.

Snapfish - www.snapfish.com - Photo books are a great way to preserve your wedding, travel, baby, or everyday memories. With lots of new designs, styles, and smart creativity tools, making one has never been easier.

Walgreens - www.Walgreens.com/Photo - Buy digital photo books at Walgreens photo center online.

Business Cards (also Stationery, Calendars, Postcards, Brochures, Letterhead, Inked Stamps)

123Print - www.123print.com - 123Print offers a wide range of products that are fully-customizable to fit the personality of any event, business, or person. At 123Print, you'll find products that help your small business stand out in a crowd, all while allowing you the freedom to stay true to yourself. We've got business cards, letterhead, memo pads, business envelopes, car magnets, rack cards, door hangers, address labels, yard signs, mailing labels, and so much more - all waiting for you to unleash your creativity!

BusinessCards.com - www.businesscards.com - Create custom designs & print your business cards, letterhead, and envelopes with our online editor. More than just an ordering system, putting creative control in your hands with powerful desktop publishing features. Start with our hundreds of layouts, graphics, logos, backgrounds, and templates pre-loaded in our editor for your business card and stationery, or upload your own backgrounds and graphics to create professional templates that can be modified for endless possibilities.

Fedex Office - www.fedex.com/us/office/designprint/index.html - Make a great impression with custom business cards.
- Choose from thousands of business card designs.
- Create online in minutes and receive in as few as 3 days.
- Make them your own with a logo, photo, and text.
- FREE 7-business-day delivery included.

Iprint - www.iprint.com - Impress clients and associates with custom business card designs.
- Optional printing on back of business cards
- Space for multiple addresses and numbers
- Design business cards in horizontal and vertical layouts
- Print business cards in larger quantities and save

Microsoft Office - office.microsoft.com/en-us/templates/ - free templates for use with Microsoft Office and Open Office.

Vistaprint - www.vistaprint.com - Vistaprint offers small businesses everything they need to market their business. We offer high-quality printed marketing materials, promotional products, and marketing services such as copywriting, design, websites, and postcard mailing.

Software

CakeBoss – www.cakeboss.com - CakeBoss is the only software *custom designed* for the home baker or small business owner! CakeBoss is unique organizational and pricing software designed to help home bakers get organized, track their costs and profits, and price their goods accurately. CakeBoss's recipe costing, pricing, organizational, and calendar features are custom-tailored to the home baker, and simply are not found in traditional accounting software. CakeBoss was designed by a cake decorator, with the specialized needs of the home baker in mind.

Wedding Cake Design Pro – www.weddingcakedesignpro.com - Wedding Cake Design Pro is completely customizable, three dimensional, and user friendly. There are no unwieldy text menus to block the view of your creation, we use graphics and buttons to make for an easy design experience. Choose from pre-set cake designs, change colors, and add embellishments and decorations as you go. Beautifully rendered images of bridal flowers are included: vibrant roses, bright daisies. Just drag it, drop it, and design it.

Miscellaneous

Office Depot - www.officedepot.com – office supplies, business cards, copying, binding

Office Max - www.officemax.com – office supplies, business cards, copying, binding

Staples - www.staples.com – office supplies, business cards, copying, binding

Uline - www.uline.com – boxes, tape, small carts, shipping and packaging materials

Publications

American Cake Decorator – www.americancakedecorating.com - Whether you are an experienced sugar artist or just learning to decorate, American Cake Decorating is your source for techniques, tips, and news. Published bimonthly. Also available in craft and cake decorating supply stores.

Mailbox News - www.americancakedecorating.com - Cake decorating is a fascinating art that captures the hearts and imaginations of those involved in it. Decorators find years of fun, excitement, and satisfaction; and Mailbox News is where decorators share their ideas and enthusiasm.

Mailbox News has been published since 1956, sharing ideas for specialty cake designs for all seasons, holidays, and occasions, and tips on decorating techniques and cake decorating news. Also, we present tried and true recipes and menus for catering events. Published bimonthly. Also available in cake decorating supply stores.

ICES Newsletter – www.ices.org - The 28-page ICES Newsletter is published eleven times a year, excluding September. It is published to keep members informed about cake decorating and relevant issues. Members are encouraged to share articles, hints, recipes, patterns, and photographs. The newsletter is mailed to all ICES members domestically and internationally at periodical rates.

Cake Central Magazine – www.cakecentral.com/magazine - This premium publication is ideal for anyone who bakes, makes cakes, aspires to make cakes, watches cake decorating shows, or has an interest in beautiful food. Ten issues per year.

Appendix A – Bride's Cake Serving Chart

To use this chart, find the number of servings you wish and follow the row to the shape of cake. A "5-7 Round" means a cake with 5" diameter and 7" diameter round tiers. This chart assumes that the top tier (smallest cake) will not be served.

Servings	Round	Square	Heart	Petal	Hexagon	Oval	Rectangle	Paisley
15	5-7			6-9				
18			6-9		6-9			
20	5-8							
20	6-8							
24		6-8						
25	5-9					5x7-7x10		
25	6-9							
25	7-9							
30	6-10							
30	7-10							
30	8-10							
32		6-9		9-12				
35	7-11							
35	8-11							
38								6-9
40	5-7-9	8-10	9-12			7x10-9x13		
45	8-12				9-12			
47				6-9-12				
50	6-8-10							
55	5-8-11							
56								9-12
58			6-9-12					
60	7-9-11	8-12						
60		9-12						
63					6-9-12			
64		6-8-10						

Servings	Round	Square	Heart	Petal	Hexagon	Oval	Rectangle	Paisley
65					9-15	5x7-7x10-9x13		
70	6-9-12							
74							9x13-11x15	
75	5-7-9-11							
75	8-10-12							
80	5-9-13							
85	7-10-13							
87				9-12-15				
92		6-9-12						
94								6-9-12
95	6-8-10-12							
95	6-10-14							
98							9x13-12x18	
100	8-11-14	8-10-12						
102				6-9-12-15				
105			9-12-15			7x10-9x13-12x16		
110					9-12-15			
115	7-9-11-13							
115	7-11-15							
120	5-8-11-14							
123			6-9-12-15					
124		6-8-10-12					7x11-9x13-11x15	
128					6-9-12-15			
130	5-7-9-11-13					5x7-7x10-9x13-12x16		
135	8-12-16							
140	8-10-12-14							
150	6-9-12-15							
160	6-8-10-12-14							
172		8-12-16						
175	7-10-13-16							

Servings	Round	Square	Heart	Petal	Hexagon	Oval	Rectangle	Paisley
184		8-10-12-14						
185	5-9-13-17							
195	7-9-11-13-15							
205	8-11-14-17							
208		6-8-10-12-14						
210	5-7-9-11-13-15							
210	6-10-14-18							
225	5-8-11-14-17							
230	8-10-12-14-16							
250	6-8-10-12-14-16							
265	6-9-12-15-18							
280	8-12-16-20							
296		8-10-12-14-16						
300	7-9-11-13-15-17							
315	5-7-9-11-13-15-17							
320		6-8-10-12-14-16						
345	8-10-12-14-16-18							
365	6-8-10-12-14-16-18							
440		8-10-12-14-16-18						
464		6-8-10-12-14-16-18						
490	8-10-12-14-16-18-20							

Appendix B – Groom's Cake Serving Chart

To use this chart, find the number of servings you wish and follow the row to the shape of cake. A "5-7 Round" means a cake with 5" diameter and 7" diameter round tiers. This chart assumes that the entire cake will be served.

Servings	Round	Square	Heart	Petal	Hexagon	Oval	Rectangle	Paisley
20				6-9				
21	5-7							
26	5-8		6-9					
27					6-9			
30	6-8							
31	5-9							
35	6-9					5-7		
36		6-8						
40	6-10							
40	7-9							
44		6-9						
45	7-10							
46	5-7-9							
47				9-12				
50	7-11							
50	8-10							
51								6-9
52				6-9-12				
55	8-11							
58			9-12					
60	6-8-10							
61	5-8-11							
63					9-12			
64		8-10						
65	8-12					7-9		
66			6-9-12					

Servings	Round	Square	Heart	Petal	Hexagon	Oval	Rectangle	Paisley
72					6-9-12			
75	7-9-11					5-7-9		
76		6-8-10						
80	6-9-12							
81	5-7-9-11							
82							7x11-9x13	
84		8-12						
86	5-9-13							
92		9-12						
94								9-12
95	8-10-12							
100	7-10-13							
102				9-12-15				
104		6-9-12						
105	6-8-10-12							
105	6-10-14							
107				6-9-12-15				6-9-12
120	8-11-14							
123			9-12-15					
124		8-10-12					9x13-11x15	
126	5-8-11-14							
128					9-12-15			
130	7-9-11-13							
130	7-11-15					7-9-12		
131			6-9-12-15					
136	5-7-9-11-13	6-8-10-12						
137					6-9-12-15			
140						5-7-9-12		
148							9x13-12x18	
155	8-12-16							
156							7x11-9x13-11x15	
160	6-9-12-15							
160	8-10-12-14							

Servings	Round	Square	Heart	Petal	Hexagon	Oval	Rectangle	Paisley
170	6-8-10-12-14							
190	7-10-13-16							
191	5-9-13-17							
196		8-12-16						
208		8-10-12-14						
210	7-9-11-13-15							
216	5-7-9-11-13-15							
220	6-10-14-18	6-8-10-12-14						
225	8-11-14-17							
231	5-8-11-14-17							
250	8-10-12-14-16							
260	6-8-10-12-14-16							
275	6-9-12-15-18							
300	8-12-16-20							
315	7-9-11-13-15-17							
320		8-10-12-14-16						
321	5-7-9-11-13-15-17							
332		6-8-10-12-14-16						
365	8-10-12-14-16-18							
375	6-8-10-12-14-16-18							
464		8-10-12-14-16-18						
476		6-8-10-12-14-16-18						
510	8-10-12-14-16-18-20							

Appendix C – Cake Serving Chart

	Circumference	Servings
Round		
5	16	6
6	19	10
7	23	15
8	25	20
9	29	25
10	32	30
11	35	35
12	38	45
13	41	55
14	45	65
15	48	80
16	51	90
17	54	105
18	57	115
20	69	145
22	72	170
24	75	195
Square		
6	25	12
8	33	24
9	37	32
10	41	40
12	49	60
14	57	84
16	65	112
18	73	144

	Circumference	Servings
Heart		
6	19	8
9	29	18
12	39	40
15	50	65
Oval		
5 X 7	21	10
7 X 10	30	25
9 X 13	37	40
12 X 16	46	65
Petal		
6	18	5
9	27	15
12	37	32
15	46	55
Hexagon		
6	18	9
9	27	18
12	36	45
15	45	65

Appendix D – Amount of Fondant Needed

Cake Size (4" high unless noted)	Size (inches)	Fondant Amount in Ounces	Cake Size (4" high unless noted)	Size (inches)	Fondant Amount in Ounces
Round	6	18	Petal	6	18
	7	21		9	30
	8	24		12	48
	9	30		15	72
	10	36	Square	6	24
	11	42		8	36
	12	48		10	48
	13	60		12	72
	14	72		14	96
	15	90		16	120
	16	108		18	144
Round (3 in. high)	6	14	Hexagon	6	18
	8	18		9	36
	10	24		12	48
	12	36		15	84
	14	48	Paisley	6x9	20
	16	72		9x12 3/4	48
Oval	7 3/4 x 5 5/8	24		12x17	72
	10 3/4 x 7 7/8	48			
	13 x 9 7/8	48			
	16 1/2 x 12 3/8	72			
Heart	6	18			
	8	26			
	9	32			
	10	36			
	12	48			
	14	72			
	15	72			
	16	96			

Appendix E – Guide to Choosing a Wedding Cake

Hand this guide out to prospective brides. They will learn a little about wedding cakes and remember you as well.

~ ~ ~

You'll probably choose only one wedding cake for yourself in a lifetime. It can be a difficult decision, along with all of your other wedding choices, but it doesn't have to be. Go with your style, whether formal or relaxed and choose what makes you happy!

When to Begin

At least four to six months before the wedding, you should start to think about the cake, choose its final design, and reserve the services of a professional.

Whom to Order From

You can order a wedding cake from the hotel or caterer responsible for the reception, hire a specialty-cake designer, or enlist the help of a talented amateur baker.

When choosing a cake designer, familiarize yourself with the designer's style by looking at photographs and tasting samples. A cake should be as delicious as it is beautiful.

Cost

The price of a wedding cake is calculated per number of servings. The more elaborate the cake, the more expensive it is. Prices range from a couple of dollars per slice for a simple cake from a local bakery to as much as $15 per slice for an exquisite cake from a celebrated designer.

A good way to reduce costs is to order a smaller cake to display, and then feed the majority of the guests from sheet cakes. This can be accomplished discreetly; after the official cake cutting, have the cake whisked away to be sliced out of sight of the guests.

Payment policies vary. It is important to get a signed contract from each cake vendor that clearly explains its policy. Most cake makers require a deposit of between 20 and 50 percent of the cost of the cake. The remainder of the payment will be due a week or two before the wedding.

Design

The design and flavor of the cake should reflect the style of the wedding as well as the bride and groom's personal taste.

A tall, heavy shape is stately and imposing, while thin, floating tiers seem airy and light.

Separating the tiers of a cake that is too thick and heavy will make it seem lighter.

One simple shape such as a dome or a cube has a strong but quiet presence.

Frosting

Buttercream is most popular for wedding cakes because it is light and delicious. Unfortunately, it may require refrigeration and does not hold up in heat. If the reception is to be outdoors in the summer, you should consider another option.

Fondant and *marzipan* are ideal for keeping larger cakes fresh when they become too large to refrigerate.

Rolled fondant has a matte finish resembling porcelain. It holds up well, and even helps to preserve a cake.

Marzipan, made of almond paste, is used in a similar manner as rolled fondant, and has a delicious and unique flavor.

Royal icing dries very hard, so it produces delicate and long-lasting decorations.

Gum paste is malleable like clay and dries hard and delicate like porcelain — ideal for realistic reproductions of fruit, flowers, and other forms.

Meringue can be used for beautiful, airy decorations and complements a cake of almost any flavor.

Decorations

A cake can be inspired by a detail of the bridal gown. Lace, ribbon or a bow, rosettes, coils of fabric, a row of buttons or pearls—any of these can be re-created in icing, gum paste, meringue, or marzipan and repeated all over the cake's surface or used as the starting point for the design.

The beauty of real flowers is unsurpassed. Use flowers that mirror the composition of the bridal bouquet or the table centerpieces. Make sure they have not been sprayed with chemicals; even so, treat flowers as garnishes unless they are specifically grown to be eaten.

Fruit can be used for a less formal effect. Fresh fruit can be coated with sugar, or miniature pears, berries, or tiny champagne grapes can be used as decoration.

Remember, a few well-chosen details may be enough, and emphasize the ones you think best express the desired style.

Flavor

A snow-white cake is traditional, but the bride and groom should feel free to choose their favorite flavor. Chocolate, lemon-poppy-seed, even carrot cakes are appearing more and more frequently at today's weddings.

Flavors have personalities, too, so try to use ones that reflect the mood of the wedding.

Chocolate is decadent, vanilla is luscious and pure, spices are autumnal, and lemon is bright and tart.

A simply-decorated cake that tastes wonderful will be as well remembered as one covered in painstakingly crafted gum-paste flowers.

~ ~ ~

Appendix F – Wedding Cake History

The first cake was a thin loaf, more bread then cake. In many cultures the cake was baked in shapes of birds or grain and used for many celebrations. In Rome, the first wedding cakes were actually loaves of wheat bread. During the ceremony, the bread was broken over the bride's head as a blessing for long life and many children. Guests often ate the crumbs as a sign of good luck.

The tiered cake symbolizes prosperity. In medieval England, wedding guests brought small cakes to the ceremony as a gift for the newlyweds. The cakes were stacked in a pile, as high as possible, to make it difficult for the newlyweds to kiss one another over the top. If the bride and groom were able to kiss over the tall stack, it was thought to symbolize a lifetime of prosperity. In the 1660s, during the reign of King Charles II, a French chef was visiting London and observed the cake piling ceremony. Appalled at the haphazard manner in which the British stacked baked goods, often to have them tumble, he conceived the idea of transforming the mountain of bland biscuits into an iced, multi-tiered cake sensation. British papers of the day are supposed to have deplored the French excess, but before the close of the century, British bakers were offering the very same magnificent creations.

The European tradition in wedding cakes is mostly white, as a symbol of purity. Wedding cakes in other cultures are often more colorful and have been a part of marriage ceremonies since medieval times. Over time, a variant of this custom evolved into the forerunner of the contemporary tiered cake that is widely used today. Although wedding cakes were once white inside and out, there are few rules about how they look today. Contemporary cakes can be any color, flavor or shape. Even if a couple prefers a traditional layered wedding cake, there are countless options for decoration.

Saving a portion of the wedding cake is an old tradition that some couples still practice. As a sign of posterity, couples freeze the top portion of their wedding cake, thawing it out on their first anniversary to share with one another. This tradition began with heavier cakes, such as fruitcakes, which are still traditional in England. Since American butter cakes won't keep this long and still taste good, many couples eat the top tier on their honeymoon or first month anniversary. A common tradition is for the baker to replicate the top tier for the couple's first anniversary.

Appendix G – Fun Facts and Wedding Statistics

Fun Facts

If an English bride passed a chimney sweep on her way to the church, and the chimney sweep kissed her, it was considered good luck.

No ceremony is complete without the kiss. In fact, there was a time when an engagement would be null and void without one. Dating back from early Roman times, the kiss represented a legal bond that sealed all contracts.

General Statistics (Ministers)

+ 175 guests are invited to an average wedding
+ Most brides (30%) plan their weddings for 7 to 12 months
+ 35% of weddings occur in the summer; 29% in the spring; 23% in the fall; 13% in the winter.
+ 11% of winter weddings are Christmas weddings
+ 53% of weddings occur in the afternoon; 31% in the evening; 16% in the morning.
+ 30% of receptions are held in churches; 20% in hotels; 20% in country clubs; and 10% each in fraternal halls, private homes, and other locations.
+ 38% of weddings have a buffet; 34% have a sit-down dinner; 28% serve only cake and punch.

Marriages by Month (Ministers)

+ January 4.7%
+ February 7.0%
+ March 6.1%
+ April 7.4%
+ May 9.8%

- June 10.8%
- July 9.7%
- August 10.3%
- September 9.6%
- October 9.4%
- November 7.4%
- December 7.8%

Appendix H – Timeline for Planning

Use this as a guide when planning your wedding cake preparations. This timeline will depend on how many cakes you have to complete, your skill level, refrigerator space, and how much room you have to build the cake.

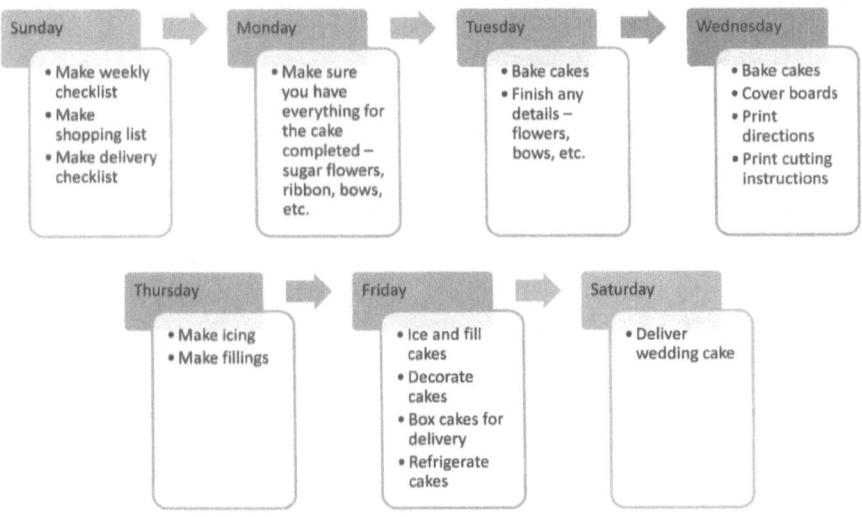

Sunday
- Make weekly checklist
- Make shopping list
- Make delivery checklist

Monday
- Make sure you have everything for the cake completed – sugar flowers, ribbon, bows, etc.

Tuesday
- Bake cakes
- Finish any details – flowers, bows, etc.

Wednesday
- Bake cakes
- Cover boards
- Print directions
- Print cutting instructions

Thursday
- Make icing
- Make fillings

Friday
- Ice and fill cakes
- Decorate cakes
- Box cakes for delivery
- Refrigerate cakes

Saturday
- Deliver wedding cake

Figure 28 – Suggested timeline

Appendix I – Example of Cake Cutting Instructions

This example was created using Microsoft PowerPoint™

Round Tiers:
Move in two inches from the tier's outer edge; cut a circle and then slice 1 in. pieces within the circle. Now move in another 2 in., cut another circle, slice 1 in. pieces and so on until the tier is completely cut. The center core of each tier and the small top tier can be cut into 3rds, 4ths, and 6ths, depending on size.

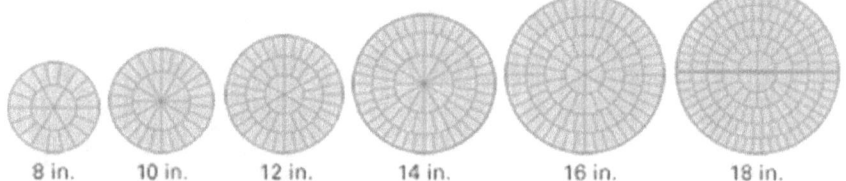

| 8 in. | 10 in. | 12 in. | 14 in. | 16 in. | 18 in. |

Size	Servings
7"	Do not cut – box provided
10"	30
13"	55

Just Desserts Georgetown · 512/930-8018

Appendix J – Graph Paper

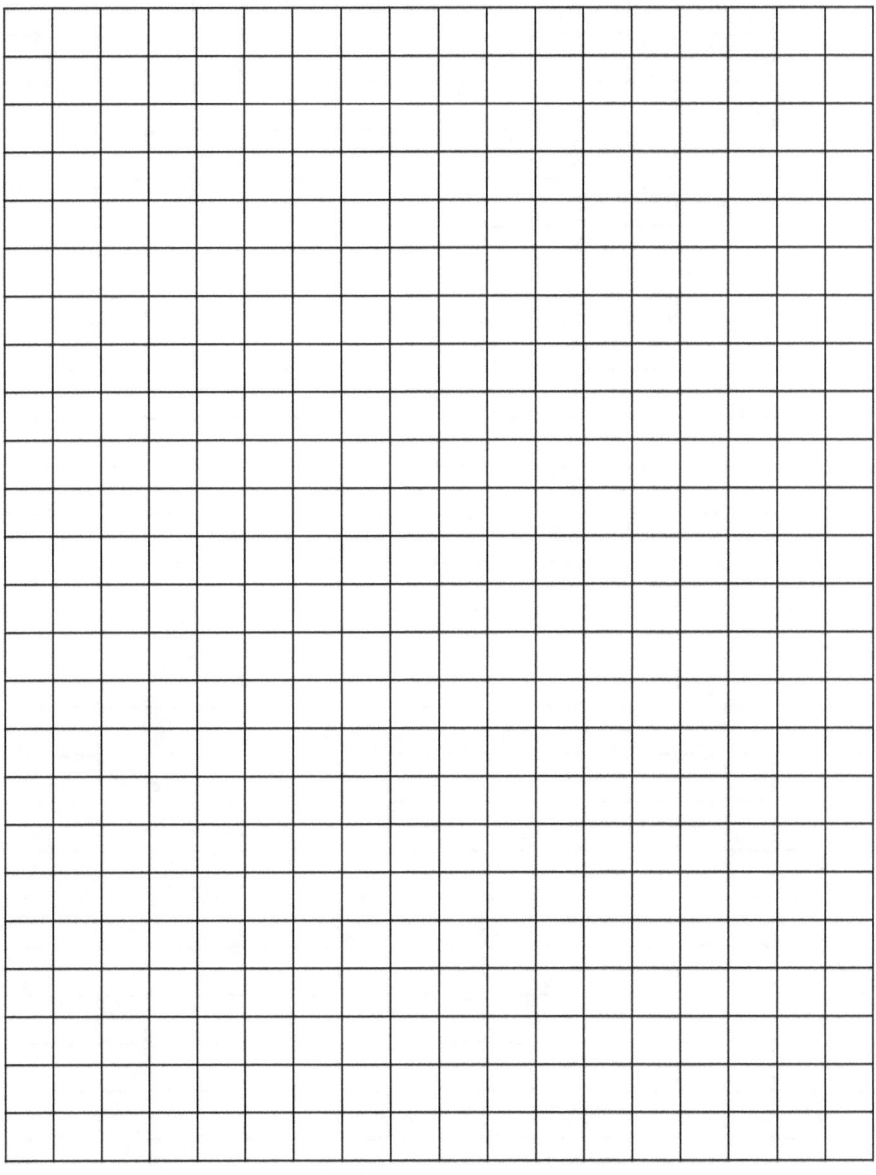

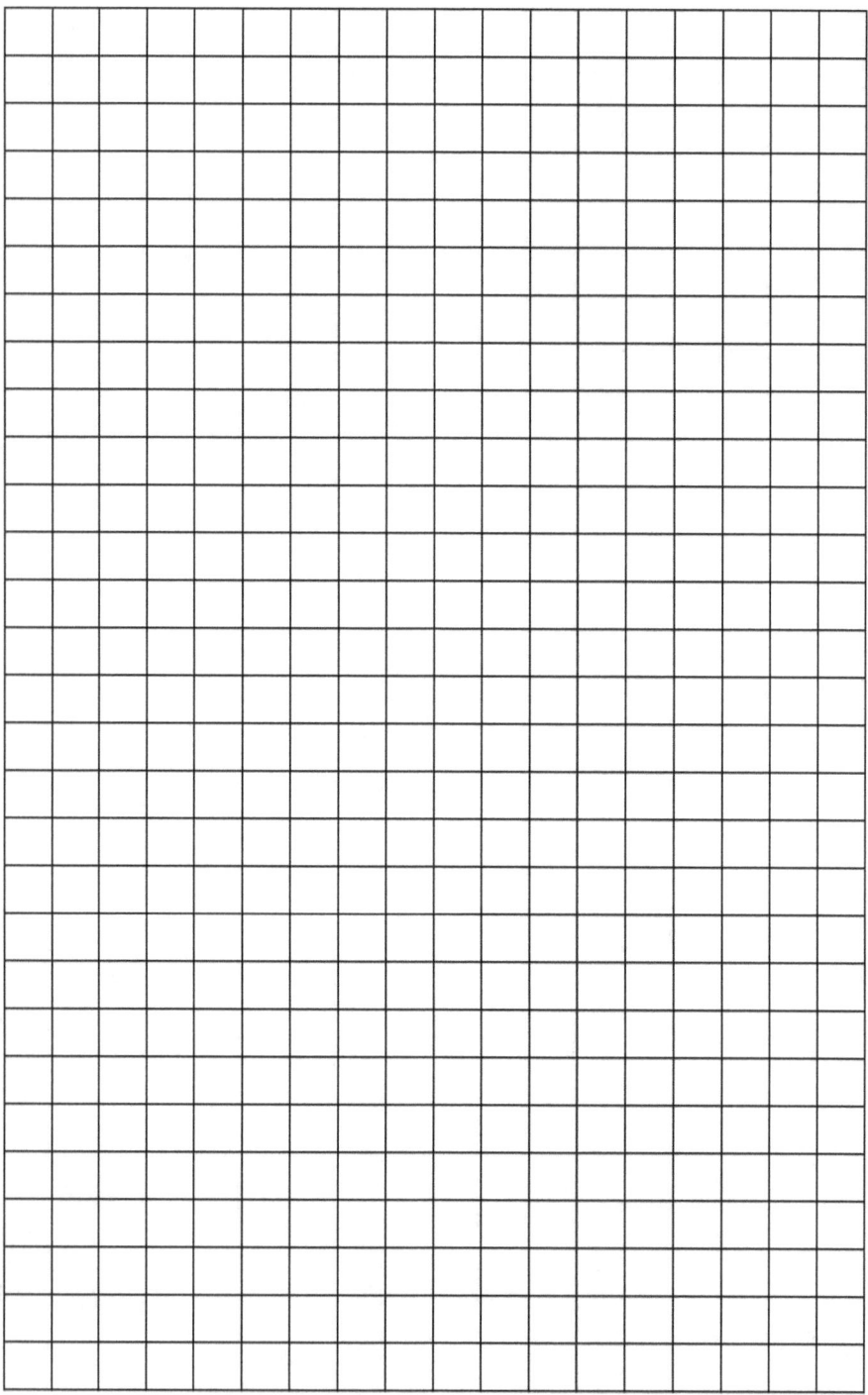

Appendix K – Sample Order Form and Contract

Wedding Order Form

Bride's Name		Phone
Bride's Email Address		2nd Phone
Groom's Name		Phone
Groom's Email Address		2nd Phone
Wedding Date/Time		Day of Week
Reception Time	Delivery Time	
Reception Contact/Phone		
Reception Location		
Reception Address		
Florist		
Photographer		
Caterer		

Cake Details

Servings	Cut Top Tier?	# Tiers/Shape
Icing Color/Type		
Cake Flavor		
Filling		
Florist Contact/Phone		
Type of Flowers/Who's Putting Flowers on Cake		
Ornament		
Notes		

Groom's Cake

Servings	Cake Flavor
Icing Color/Type	Filling

Miscellaneous		Totals	
Ornament		Price of Cake	
Stand Rental		Miscellaneous Total	
Fountain Rental			
		Total	
Miscellaneous Total		Amount Paid	
Stand Deposit		Amount Due	
Fountain Deposit		Cancellation Date	

129

PROJECT DESCRIPTION: The cake to be provided for the Event by _____ is described in the attached order. Any changes to this existing order: size, design, flavor, or filling etc. will be accepted until ten (10) calendar days prior to the Event (Cancellation Date). Any changes made less than ten (10) calendar days prior to the event date (Cancellation Date) cannot be guaranteed

PAYMENT ARRANGEMENT: To secure your event date, _____ will decline other work. Accordingly, you agree to the following payment arrangement:

- A deposit of 50% of the total contract price is due upon signing this contract, of which $50.00 is non-refundable within ten (10) calendar days of the Event (Cancellation Date). If the deposit is not received, other work may be contracted, releasing your requested date. The $50.00 deposit is subtracted from your balance due. On cakes totaling less than $100.00, the deposit will be one half of the total order.
- The remainder of the total price shall be due ten (10) calendar days before the Event.
- Credit card payments are welcome through PayPal. The PayPal address is _____
- If payment has not been received, we reserve the right to refuse your order.
- Deposit and Rental items must be returned by seven (7) calendar days following your event date or your deposit will be retained. Date items due _____.
- All returned checks will be subject to a $20.00 handling fee, as charged by the bank.

| _____ | | _____ |
| *Signature* | | *Date* |

| _____ | | _____ |
| *Signature* | | *Date* |

www.ingramcontent.com/pod-product-compliance
Lightning Source LLC
Chambersburg PA
CBHW051418280526
45785CB00003B/1073